TRACY Y. CANNON

Tracy Y. Cannon

TRACY Y. CANNON

TABERNACLE ORGANIST & PIONEERING MUSICIAN

1879–1961

SHELBY FISHER

SIGNATURE BOOKS | 2026 | SALT LAKE CITY

For Elinore, Charlotte, and Caroline

Join our mail list at www.signaturebooks.com for details on events and related titles we think you'll enjoy.

Design by Jason Francis

FIRST EDITION | 2026

Paperback ISBN: 978-1-56085-531-6
Ebook ISBN: 978-1-56085-509-5

CONTENTS

INTRODUCTION

On a cold day in late November 1908, twenty-nine-year-old Tracy Young Cannon stepped off the train in Salt Lake City, returning to his bustling hometown following two years of musical study in Europe with some of the continent's most renowned pedagogues. Cannon arrived armed with the latest training in music theory and organ performance, along with a newly acquired polish garnered from exposure to Western Europe's most cosmopolitan cultural centers. Having shed at least some of his provinciality, Cannon felt hopeful about his future as a young musician, particularly as a church musician, and he was brimming with ideas for how best to improve the caliber of music within the youthful LDS Church.

Cannon's optimistic fervor was shared by many in Salt Lake City at the turn of the century. Beginning with the 1890 Manifesto, which urged church members to heed the "law of the land" regarding marriage and abstain from entering into new polygamous unions, LDS Church president Wilford Woodruff had ushered in a new era of Mormonism which rejected its previous isolationist tendencies and instead began the painstaking process of retrofitting Mormon culture to dovetail with broader American society. This transformation lasted for several decades and destabilized Utah's theocratic foundations, upon which had been built the state's church-controlled political parties, schools, industries, and financial systems. Gradually, the church loosened (without relinquishing) its tightly held grip on the state's politics and economy. In the process, it joined the wider progressive Social Gospel movement by aligning with national political parties, encouraging women's suffrage, creating a public school system overseen by state governing bodies rather than the church, and espousing the view that education and innovation could cure society's woes. Heber J. Grant proclaimed in 1930, "The past 100 years have seen more development in science, medicine, mechanical arts, tolerance and religion than any previous period in history. Never has the growth of the scientific attitude been so marked as during the period from 1830 to 1930."

While some abhorred this embrace of external forces, others saw the church's modernization as fulfillment of prophecy, for the prophets had declared, "The keys of the kingdom of God are committed unto man on the earth, and from thence shall the gospel roll forth unto the ends of the earth, as the stone which is cut out of the mountain without hands shall roll forth, until it has filled the whole earth." In the minds of the LDS faithful, the restored gospel was the missing keystone that would complete the trifecta of education, innovation, and "true" religion, spreading Zion's light and truth among the nations of the earth.

Cannon fully embraced this Zionist vision with both zeal and steadfastness, writing in 1905: "I see that the possibilities for the development of music are great in our Church, yes, greater than among any people on earth. God's prophets have predicted that they would become the greatest people on earth and so they shall. Music will be one of the branches of learning in which they will excel." Unlike the Mormon music of Cannon's predecessors, which was "folksy" and approachable, Cannon's vision for the modern music of Zion was one of elegance and civility, which borrowed liberally from the musical traditions of both the Anglican and Lutheran arms of the Protestant Reformation.

Cannon was not a disruptive innovator, but rather a reformer and modernizer; like the stone cut from the mountain, his vision of LDS music was fully formed and needed only the steady hand of refinement. To realize this vision required two things: a comprehensive educational system which would equip the Saints not only to sing and play such a demanding repertoire, but also to appreciate sacred music which ran obliquely against its secular counterparts; and a thoroughly defined collection of music which would encompass hymnody, choral, and instrumental works. This ambitious plan spanned nearly the entirety of Cannon's fifty-year career, during which Cannon remained not only steadfastly committed to his objective, but tirelessly confident in the capacity of church members to fulfill his vision for the music of Zion.

CHAPTER ONE

"I AM A MUSICIAN BECAUSE I JUST HAD TO BE ONE"

Tracy Cannon, born Tracy Young Croxall, was the sixth child of Mark Croxall and Caroline Partridge Young, a daughter of Brigham Young. Croxall was a practicing polygamist with three additional wives: Mary Eliza Young, another daughter of Brigham Young, and a pair of sisters who were immigrants from Denmark. Cannon's parents divorced when he was young leaving him with few memories of his father. In 1951, Cannon recalled:

> Of the events of [my father's] early life I know nothing definite. He possessed unusual musical talent and by the time he reached maturity he had become quite proficient as a cornetist. The musical quality of his tone was outstanding and he was in great demand as a soloist in public and [musical] gatherings. Whenever he played a song as a solo he always very thoroughly studied the words of the song, just as a good singer would do. His playing thus became very expressive and his interpretive ability, coupled with his beautiful tone, made him the most popular cornetist in Utah. Many people who heard him play have told me they had never heard anyone play the cornet whose tone was as beautiful as the tone my father produced.[1]

In 1884, Cannon's mother remarried, becoming the seventh wife of George Q. Cannon. Tracy and his siblings took the Cannon surname and moved to the family farm, located on the west side of Salt

1. Mark Croxall was a member of the Salt Lake Theater Orchestra, where he worked closely with many of the city's musical elite including Joseph J. Daynes, Ebenezer Beesley, and C. J. Thomas. Tracy Y. Cannon, Papers, 1899–1961, Church History Library, Church of Jesus Christ of Latter-day Saints, Salt Lake City (hereafter, CHL).

Lake City. On the farm were several houses, in addition to barns and a schoolhouse that George Q. Cannon built to educate his forty-three children. Cannon recalled his childhood on the farm writing, "As I look back to my childhood days, I see the beginnings of this sorrow and struggle in my disposition to be extremely sensitive ... my sensitiveness was probably intensified because of an affliction in my right eye, and also because my hair was red and my face freckled, and because the boys did not hesitate to call attention to these things."[2]

Cannon showed interest in music as a young child recalling: "I am a musician because I just had to be one. It started when I received a toy violin for Christmas when I was four or five years old. From then on I was constantly teased to be a musician, but my mother was opposed because of the temptations that faced a night-playing orchestral musician."[3]

As fate would have it, orchestral music was not in Cannon's future. At the age of 16, he was appointed choir director of the newly organized Cannon Ward. Shortly thereafter, Cannon began to study piano, organ, and harmony with John J. McClellan, an instructor at LDS College in Salt Lake City who had recently completed his studies and a brief teaching stint at the University of Michigan in Ann Arbor. Cannon spoke highly of his association with McClellan, calling it "a treasured experience;" however, opportunities for advanced music instruction were scarce in turn-of-the-century Utah and it was necessary for serious students like Cannon to seek a university or conservatory education in the east or Europe.[4] George Q. Cannon and Caroline met with McClellan in April 1898 to discuss Cannon's prospects:

> Tracy is desirous of going to Germany to get instruction in music. Brother McClellan, I understand, has favored this movement. I have been desirous to know his views concerning Tracy and his fitness for the profession of music. I questioned him very closely on this point, as to whether he was sufficiently advanced now to go, and whether if he did go he thought he would make a first class musician. I told him

2. Carol Hinckley Cannon, "Tracy Y. Cannon: His Life and His Legacy," 1979, CHL.

3. Cannon Papers.

4. Cannon Papers.

> that we did not wish him to be a second or third rate man, nor to adopt a profession at which he could not succeed. In answer, he said that he thought him sufficiently advanced to go to Germany and continue his studies; he considered him an excellent student, and though perhaps not so quick as some, yet he was very solid and thorough. His knowledge of harmony was very good, and he thought he would make a fine composer, and that he was safe in adopting music as a profession. He said, that which he hoped was that he and Tracy might be companions hereafter. He spoke in very high terms of the boy; and after hearing what he said, we felt more satisfied – at least, I did – as to the propriety of his going to Germany, if we could raise the means to send him.[5]

In September 1898 George Q. Cannon, a prolific journal keeper, noted that Cannon seemed to have settled on Ann Arbor for music study, probably with the encouragement of McClellan.[6] Shortly thereafter at the age of nineteen, Cannon left for Michigan.

Cannon's primary piano instructor at Ann Arbor was Alberto Jonás, a Spanish-born piano virtuoso and student of Russian pianist Anton Rubinstein. Cannon wrote little about his studies with Jonás; however, other students recalled Jonás's exacting nature and insistence upon slow mastery of each piece's details.[7] Cannon's organ instruction was under Albert Stanley, who was professor of music and co-founder of the University Music Society (which later became the University of Michigan School of Music). Stanley was also instrumental in the university's acquisition of the 3,901-pipe Farrand & Votey organ, originally built for the 1893 World's Columbian Exposition held in Chicago. Christened the Frieze Memorial Organ after Stanley's friend and colleague the late Henry Simmons Frieze, the entire instrument was crated, shipped, and rebuilt in Ann Arbor following the Exposition. As university organist Stanley gave regular organ recitals; when Stanley was not available, McClellan often filled in.[8] The Frieze organ as reported by McClellan was no doubt an attractive prospect to Cannon.

5. George Q. Cannon, April 21, 1898, *The Journal of George Q. Cannon*, churchhistorianspress.org.

6. George Q. Cannon, *Journal*, September 13, 1898.

7. Ross Edillor Salvosa, "Alberto Jonás' Master School and Its Role in Early Twentieth-Century Piano Virtuosity (PhD diss., University of British Columbia, 2018).

8. Richard R. Lyman, *Conference Reports of the Church of Jesus Christ of Latter-day Saints, 1897–2017* (1925), 122.

Following the end of his first year, Cannon returned to Salt Lake City for the summer. He wasted no time putting his freshly honed skills to work directing the Sunday School singing and the choir of the Cannon Ward. He also organized a sight-singing class for ward members, writing: "I did not charge them anything for the instruction I gave them and if they can sing the songs of Zion better than they could before taking the course, I will be satisfied. If I can do nothing more than raise the standard of our church music and teach young people how to sing good music, I will be satisfied."[9]

In the fall, Cannon returned to Ann Arbor for his second year of study. He rented two upstairs rooms for $1 per week, plus a "new Ludwig piano" at the rate of $5 per month. He continued with organ, piano, and counterpoint lessons and attended faculty concerts. Many years later, Cannon recalled working hard during his second year, rising at 5:15 in the morning and retiring at 9:30 in the evening every day except Sunday. His journal entries also tell of feelings of discouragement and "the blues," and also of homesickness, particularly for a "certain lovely maid" back in Utah. In December, Cannon's longing for home intensified after receiving a Christmas package and news that his grandmother had passed away. At the turn of the new year, Cannon played for his first non-LDS worship service: "Today I played the organ in the Congregational church and I suppose did well considering everything. It was the first time I had done the work and I did not know I would play today until yesterday morning so it took a great deal of hard work to get all the music up. Will receive $3 for the work. I am going to try to get a position in some church if I can."[10] He also reported trouble with his eyes, a problem that would continue to hamper his playing in the years to follow.

Cannon prepared to return to Salt Lake City after completing his second year in Ann Arbor in June 1900 having decided to remain home for a year to regain his physical strength and save money: "Tomorrow I have my last lessons for this year and then I will be through with this place for this year and perhaps forever, who knows. I received a letter from Mother today and she said she could hardly see how I could come back next year unless I could get a church

9. Cannon, "Tracy Y. Cannon."
10. Cannon, "Tracy Y. Cannon."

position or something to help myself financially and I have no position in sight at present."[11]

Cannon did not make any journal entries for one year following his return to Salt Lake City. An advertisement placed in the *Deseret News* in November 1900 indicates that he had taken a studio at Calder Music and was presumably teaching harmony and piano. In June 1901, Cannon recorded the death of his stepfather George Q. Cannon on April 13 as well as his call to serve as a missionary for the LDS Church in England.

11. Cannon, "Tracy Y. Cannon."

CHAPTER TWO

"NOW I AM FAMOUS"

Cannon began his service as a missionary on July 9, 1901, at a special meeting held in the Salt Lake Temple Annex before embarking on his journey to England. He arrived in Liverpool on July 25 before traveling on to London. Street meetings and door-to-door "tracting" were the preferred methods of proselytizing in London at the turn of the century. Anti-Mormon sentiment was strong in 1901, encouraged by news of the church's case argued before the Supreme Court in 1890 (which had upheld the Edmunds-Tucker Act and disincorporated the LDS Church), the B. H. Roberts trial, and by a general fear that Mormon missionaries came to England to convert single young women into polygamy. Cannon, still demonstrating his boyhood reservation, expressed distaste for tracting, noting, "I have about come to the conclusion that I was not made to do tracting. I can't learn to like it. It is almost impossible for me to get conversations. I don't know how to start a conversation and it seems I can't learn. My mind seems to be a blank when I try to talk."[1]

Nevertheless, Cannon estimated that he distributed over 21,000 tracts over the course of his mission. In addition to pamphlets, Cannon also left copies of the Book of Mormon with investigators, which he would return to collect later in the week.

Cannon was a diligent missionary, often retiring late in the evening and rising early. His eyes continued to aggravate him, and he suffered from frequent headaches. Lack of money was a near constant concern for him. In spite of Cannon's worries, he found opportunities to play the piano and organ, sing, and direct choirs;

1. Tracy Y. Cannon, "Mission Journal" (1901–1905), MS 14556, CHL.

he was often called upon to supply music for meetings and other gatherings, though locating instruments for practice was an issue. Cannon's best option was to rent "time" at music stores, if there was an organ or piano available: "I went to all the music stores in the neighborhood trying to find a place to practice. But English music stores are so behind the times. I did not succeed in finding one until I had been to about 12 stores. I finally found a place down by Hackney Station where I can practice by paying six pence per hour."[2]

He also attended numerous cultural events at the Royal Opera House, Royal Albert Hall, Westminster Abbey, and the Cathedral of Saint Paul. A visit to the Royal College of Music in 1902 had a profound impact on Cannon, and he spent considerable time observing the workings of the college, even meeting with an administrator: "It gave me the old longing to again be in music up to my neck and I had a feeling of regret that my eyes would not permit my continuing musical studies. But I must take conditions as they are and make the best of something else, what it will be I know not. However, whatever I do I will not and cannot altogether keep away from music. I only hope I can leave it alone enough to be able to make a living at something else."[3]

It was not uncommon at the turn of the century for missionaries to seek permission to travel outside mission boundaries. Cannon did just that, traveling to Berlin where he attended a conference and visited several of his brothers who were living abroad. A number of music students with roots in Utah were living in Berlin at the time, and Cannon attended events including performances of the Royal Orchestra and the opera, under the baton of Richard Strauss. This visit seemed to have reignited Cannon's desire to study music in Berlin, "I received an excellent letter from dear Mother. She says that if she can afford it and my eyes are strong enough that she wants me to spend six months to a year in Germany to study music and language."[4]

The solace Cannon found in music did not extend to all areas of his missionary service. Mormonism's more controversial beliefs were frequently the subject of local newspaper coverage, and Cannon

2. Cannon, Mission Journal.
3. Cannon, Mission Journal.
4. Cannon, Mission Journal.

faced hostility from some Londoners. Cannon reported that he was often questioned about polygamy, yet he steadfastly refused to engage in arguments, writing, "Yes, we are not sent out here to teach it, and it is not taught nor practiced at home. But I did not say that I did not believe it because I believe every doctrine that has been or is a part of [the] gospel as I understand it."[5]

Cannon's journal betrays the complicated position of the church on polygamy during this period. As the Smoot hearings progressed in the spring of 1904 he wrote: "We advertised [the conference] quite extensively and, as the Smoot Investigation was receiving attention in the London papers, a number of reporters from *The Daily Express, The Daily Mail, The Daily Mirror, The Chronicle, The Daily News,* and others called and interviewed us. There was much space devoted to us.... We elders spoke quite freely to the reporters, too freely I fear, and in a way they gave us fair reports, although they changed what we said to make it sensational."[6]

Somewhere in the course of these interviews, a reporter learned that Cannon was the grandson of polygamous leader Brigham Young and called on the mission house for an interview. On April 8, 1904, just two days after Joseph F. Smith issued the "Second Manifesto" denouncing polygamy, an article appeared in the London tabloid *The Daily Mirror.* The paper condemned the church's immoral practices and demanded that laws be used against the missionaries, "whose object is without a doubt to entice young girls and women to live an immoral life."[7] The article then cast doubt on the missionaries' emphatic declaration that polygamy was not taught or practiced in Utah, stating, "Whatever the creed preached by the Mormon missionaries at present in London, there is no doubt whatever that polygamy is rampant in Utah." As the report luridly stated:

> Mr. Tracy Young Cannon, Brigham Young's grandson, was questioned by a *Mirror* representative as to the existence of polygamy in Salt Lake City.
>
> "I can solemnly affirm," he stated, "that no polygamous marriage has been solemnized by the Mormon Church since 1888, when the

5. Cannon, Mission Journal.
6. Cannon, Mission Journal.
7. "Mormons and Polygamy," *Daily Mirror,* April 8, 1904.

law prohibiting bigamy was enforced. At the present time polygamy is banned by the Mormon Church, owing to a revelation from the Lord forbidding it."

"When was this revelation made," Mr. Cannon was asked; "after the Act of Congress was passed?"

"Yes," replied the Mormon.

"Then, why, if polygamy, as you state, was forbidden by Divine revelation, do you still regard it as a Divine principle?" was a further interrogation. No explanation was forthcoming to this statement of a paradoxical situation.

"Have any polygamous marriages been secretly performed since 1888?" was the last question.

"Not to my knowledge," was the reply.

Recent revelations in America prove that Mr. Cannon is very ill-informed, or willfully blind, to the condition of things in the Mormon community, for it is well established that the only difference in the situation in Salt Lake City before 1888 and at the present time is that now polygamous marriages are secretly performed instead of openly as before the prohibiting Act was passed.[8]

Cannon received the article with a wry humor writing:

> Now I am famous! Wonder upon wonder ... I went to bed unknown and forlorn and woke up to find myself talked about by all the people of great London. And to think that I had this great fortune come to me through the beneficent kindness of the wonderful, unsensational, conservative, accurate, truthful 'Mirror' ... Through the free advertising the papers had given us, the week following our conference we had a number of strangers at our Sunday school and the hall meeting was so crowded that night that there was not even standing room ... Our meetings have been very well attended since and we have made many new friends.[9]

Cannon's interaction with the media seems to have emboldened him; he wrote of preaching with increased confidence. Having finally settled into the routine of preaching, visiting, and tracting, he completed his missionary service uneventfully. Cannon received word that his mother had passed away in late 1903, which amplified his

8. "Mormons and Polygamy."
9. Cannon, Mission Journal.

feelings of loneliness and homesickness. When he finally returned home in April 1904, Cannon calculated that his missionary service had cost him $1,146.25, but from it he had gained "much useful experience."[10]

10. Cannon, Mission Journal.

CHAPTER THREE

"MY AIM IS TO BECOME A THOROUGH MUSICIAN"

The family home on Cannon Farm had been sold after the death of George Q. Cannon, so following his return from England to the United States in 1904, Cannon lived with his sister Ada and her husband. Deeply frustrated by the continued pain in his eyes which impeded his ability to read music notation, Cannon contemplated his career path:

> I was worried as to what to do for a living. I had decided to give up music as a profession and as I could see nothing else to do, I felt very unhappy and unsettled. However, after talking with John McClellan and others, I came to the conclusion that music was the thing for me and I could teach without a very great strain on my eyes. I accordingly procured room 28 in the Manox Building at 24 E. South Temple Street for $7 a month and opened a studio in July 1904. And here I am yet. I have had fair success ... I have taken in from $20 to $60 a month so I have not starved.[1]

In an attempt to further establish himself in the community as a music teacher, Cannon, along with several colleagues including McClellan, organized the Utah School of Music in Salt Lake City. The group pooled their resources, each contributing $20 to produce a catalog and newspaper advertisements. Cannon had long been concerned with raising "the standard of our church music," a sentiment which is evident in an entry from *The Salt Lake Telegram:* "An organization to be known as the Utah School of Music has been effected

1. Carol Hinckley Cannon,"Tracy Y. Cannon: His Life and His Legacy," 1979, CHL.

in this city by a number of the best-known artists of Utah. The purpose of the enterprise is to fill the need for a first-class conservatory, which has long been felt in this part of the country."[2] The venture was not a success, however, and Cannon reported that they "got no visible results for [their] money."[3]

The following year at the April 1905 general conference of the church, Cannon was named as assistant Salt Lake Tabernacle organist where he would serve alongside McClellan, who had been named as principal organist in 1901. At that time, Cannon's position was a true calling, meaning it was done without compensation and it was assumed that organists would have gainful employment elsewhere. The appointment did bring Cannon notoriety however, which presumably boosted his teaching and social prospects. "My work on the organ has been a great help. It has put my name before the public very much and has given me much pleasure besides, as the Tabernacle organ is a glorious instrument. I have given a number of public recitals when McClellan has been away and have accompanied the choir a few times."[4]

In the month following his appointment as assistant organist, Cannon became engaged to Elsie Riter, whose family lived not far from Ada's home in Salt Lake City. Elsie was the daughter of William W. Riter, a prominent Utah financier and entrepreneur, and his wife, Priscilla Jennings. The wedding was initially planned for the following year, allowing Cannon to become more established in his career before assuming financial responsibility for a family; however, Cannon had made plans to travel to Europe for extended study with Jonás at the Klindworth-Scharwenka Conservatory in Berlin and Alexandre Guilmant in Paris (a trip sponsored by the Riters).[5] Thus the wedding was moved up to September so that Elsie could accompany Cannon to Europe. Cannon gave up his teaching studio

---

2. "Utah School of Music Organized," *Salt Lake Telegram,* August 13, 1904.

3. Cannon, "Tracy Y. Cannon."

4. Cannon, "Tracy Y. Cannon."

5. The Klindworth–Scharwenka Conservatory was a merger between the Klindworth Musikschule, opened by German pianist Karl Klindworth and the Scharwenka music school, founded by Polish pianist Xaver Scharwenka. It was an internationally recognized conservatory that produced a number of concert pianists. McClellan had studied piano with Scharwenka in Berlin from 1899 to 1900.

in order to make preparations for both the wedding and the voyage overseas. He recorded in his journal:

> Two weeks from today I am to marry Elsie Riter in the Salt Lake Temple.... We will have a large reception that night at the Riter's. We have sent out 200 invitations and expect about 300 to be present ...John J. McClellan has been in Portland with the Ogden Tabernacle choir recently and while he was away I have had the organ. I played three public recitals and I played at the services two Sundays. I did better than I have ever done before and received many compliments for my work. I feel that I have made much progress on the organ this summer. I love this organ and shall miss it greatly while away. I hope I shall not be denied the pleasure of playing on it when I return again. I am now busy getting ready for the wedding and also for going away. We expect to leave a day or two after the wedding for Berlin where I am going to study music for two or three years.... In regard to Elsie, I feel I am getting a wife that will be all to me a wife should be. I feel we shall be happy together. We may both have faults, but my desire is that we shall both be charitable and forgiving and help each other to become better.[6]

About one week prior to the wedding, Elsie suffered a gastrointestinal attack (presumed to be food poisoning) from which she never fully recovered. The wedding proceeded, but Elsie remained weak. Cannon was once again recognized as assistant Tabernacle organist at the October 1905 general conference. He was immediately granted a leave of absence and on October 10, 1905, Cannon and Elsie left Salt Lake City for New York where they boarded a steamer bound for Hamburg. By November, the newlyweds were settled in Berlin, having taken a small flat, and Cannon had resumed his studies with Jonás. For a time, Cannon seemed content; on the final day of 1905 he recorded in his journal:

> Today is the last day of the most eventful year of my life. I am married to the dearest, sweetest, and best girl in all the world. I am also in Berlin studying under the great master, Jonas, and have at last realized the great ambition to study music in Germany. My desire now is that I may be able to remain with Jonás for two years from now, then to go to Paris and study organ for six months, and return home in time to start

6. Cannon, "Tracy Y. Cannon."

> teaching in Salt Lake in 1908 ... my aim is to become a thorough musician in the broadest sense, not merely a piano or organ player.[7]

He also expressed a desire to continue his work as a church musician rather than a secular one, an impulse he had first expressed as a student at Ann Arbor, "I have had a plan in my mind for years for the betterment of music in our Church. If I ever carry it out, I shall have to first become big myself. That is one reason why I want to be a thorough musician."[8]

Elsie's mother and two sisters arrived in Berlin in the summer with plans to tour Europe alongside the Cannons. Elsie became ill in Rome with "gastric fever," requiring the attention of a trained nurse and delaying the travel party for two weeks. Her health continued to decline, so she and Cannon returned to Berlin while the rest of the Riters continued their tour. By the spring of 1907, Elsie was gravely ill and Cannon made arrangements for her to travel to Salt Lake City where she could recuperate surrounded by her family. This was not to be, however, and Elsie passed away in Berlin on May 27, 1907. Heartbroken, Cannon brought her remains back to Utah for burial.

In late summer of 1907, Cannon returned to Berlin to complete his studies thanks in part to the financial support of his late wife's parents, though the experience was clouded in grief: "No one can ever know the sorrow of my life in coming back to Berlin where we had our happy little home together. I have no ambition to study. It seems I can only think of Elsie."[9]

Cannon was part of a rather large group of expat students, musicians, and missionaries from Utah who were living and studying in Berlin. He completed his studies with Jonás in the spring of 1908 and then left for Paris to study organ with Alexandre Guilmant and composition with Albert Roussel. Guilmant was widely acclaimed as a concert organist and improviser. He was the first French organist to tour the United States and played a series of forty recitals in Festival Hall at the Louisiana Purchase Exposition, held in Saint Louis, Missouri, in 1904. *The Salt Lake Tribune* reported on Guilmant's exposition recitals:

7. Cannon, "Tracy Y. Cannon."
8. Cannon, "Tracy Y. Cannon."
9. Cannon, "Tracy Y. Cannon."

> It is a matter of keen regret that Salt Lakers did not have the opportunity to hear Alexandre Guilmant, the great French organist, who has been filling a series of engagements at Festival Hall, St. Louis. Those who had the pleasure of hearing the great French organist and composer play at St. Louis feel the disappointment the more keenly as his wonderful handling of the organ in Festival Hall—which impresses one with its bigness rather than its quality of tone—but made greater the desire to hear him manipulate the keys of the Tabernacle organ.[10]

Guilmant's American tours secured his popularity in the United States, both as a composer and as a pedagogue, and American organists such as Cannon clamored for the opportunity to study with the musical giant. Guilmant's organ sonatas and other short compositions were staples of the daily Tabernacle recital programs during the early 1900s.

Cannon made no journal entries during his time with Guilmant; however, in 1908 he wrote an extensive letter which was published in the *Deseret News* under the headline, "Salt Lake Pupil of Guilmant Describes the Great Organist." Cannon's letter details not only the particulars of his studies but also eloquently communicates his deep admiration for Guilmant:

> Paris, May 11— Probably there is no organist in America who has not admired the compositions of Alexander Guilmant; certainly there is no name of the present day associated with the organ that stands out with more prominence than his. Indirectly he has influenced the advancement of organ playing in America to a great extent, because a large number of our best organists have been pupils of his; and no one can come under his influence without becoming convinced that the name Guilmant stands for all that is best in the organist's world.... Although now 71 years old he has not lessened his activities. While he no longer plays at La Trinité he has other duties that keep him very busy. He is a professor at the Conservatoire, organist of the "Societe des Concerts," member of the "Consieut Superieure du Conservatoire," professor at the Scola Cantorum, etc. Besides all this, he is constantly filling concert engagements and teaching. It is difficult to see where he finds time for composing.... Guilmant has built himself a beautiful villa in Meudon, a suburb of Paris, and it is here that he works. In his music room, which

10. "Music Notes," *Salt Lake Tribune,* October 23, 1904.

by the way, is a small sized concert hall, is a beautifully toned three manual Cavaillé-Coll organ, built after his own design, also two grand pianos and two reed organs.... He has a large class of pupils at the present time. They come to him from all parts of the world. The other day the writer asked him how many American pupils he had had. "Oh, I cannot say," he replied, with a wave of the hand, which indicated that the number has been too large to remember.... We students go to his home each week one hour before the appointed time for the lesson, and practice on a small one manual pipe organ, which is located in another part of the house. When we meet our teacher he always greets us with a smile and asks: "Avez vous bien travaille?" ("Have you worked well?"). After showing him what we have brought to play he arranges the proper registration for us and we begin our lesson. We must play something of Bach each time, either three or four chorales or a fugue. Then we always have something of his own, either a movement or two of one of his sonatas or a smaller piece. He insists on a perfect legato, and is very particular about repeating repeated notes. He expects the pupil to play each piece just as it is written. If it be very difficult, he will let him play it the first time as slowly as he may desire, but no wrong note must be struck and each note must have its proper value. He always plays for us the most important pieces we are studying. And what an inspiration it is to hear him play! ... It is not possible for the writer to convey in words his admiration for M. Guilmant's genius, both as composer and performer. He has reached the top round of the organist's ladder and although he has now reached the age when most men are ready to give up the active battle of life, he still remains, in the writer's opinion, the king of all organists.[11]

It was during this youthful period that Cannon first tried his own hand at composition, writing a series of pieces for voice and piano which he later referred to as "art songs." This appellation is quite generous, as the songs have more in common with Tin Pan Alley love songs and novelties than the art songs of Schubert. Cannon used texts by popular authors such as Lucy Maud Montgomery, as well as original poetry by his half-brother Georgius, who was thirteen years his junior. The venture seemed to be purely pecuniary and impersonal, as even the death of Elsie, which for other musicians

11. "Salt Lake Pupil of Guilmant Describes the Great Organist," *Deseret News,* May 30, 1908.

may have prompted some sort of emotionally driven compositions, elicited not so much as a dedication. The song series was never published and by 1912 Cannon had abandoned the composition of secular music entirely.[12]

Cannon returned from Europe to Salt Lake City in November 1908 and resumed teaching at the start of the new year, advertising that he would be accepting pupils of piano, organ, and composition at the Templeton Building.[13] Cannon was also organist at First Congregational Church of Salt Lake (then located at the intersection of 100 South and 400 East and possessing an organ built by Farrand and Votey), serving there from 1909 until sometime in 1912. He continued to live with his sister Ada and her husband William and remained on good terms with the Riters where he was a frequent dinner guest.[14] In 1909, Cannon had resumed his duties as assistant organist at the Salt Lake Tabernacle, along with Edward P. Kimball who also served as assistant.[15] McClellan remained principal organist. Fortunately for Cannon and Kimball, the position now came with a modest salary.

In addition to teaching and performing in Salt Lake City, Cannon also began to teach music lessons at the church's Weber Academy in Ogden, Utah, often using Ogden First Congregational Church as a recital venue for his students. In 1910 he began courting a young woman from Ogden, Lettie Taylor, who was the daughter of Richard James and Sarah Farr Taylor.[16] Lettie recalled that Cannon telephoned her nearly every time he came to Ogden, often sending flowers or candy. Cannon's position as a Tabernacle organist gave him an air of celebrity, and Lettie was "flattered that one of the organists

12. Cannon's unpublished scores are included in his papers held by the Church History Library.

13. "Tracy Cannon," *Deseret News*, November 7, 1908.

14. William was the son of George Q. Cannon and his third polygamous wife, Eliza Tenney.

15. Edward Kimball was made assistant organist in 1906.

16. Richard was the son of church president John Taylor and Jane Ballantyne, Taylor's third wife. Taylor had baptized the parents of George Q. Cannon in England (Taylor's first wife was George Q. Cannon's aunt, Leonora). After George Q. Cannon's mother died on the ship en route to the United States, Taylor took Cannon into his home as a printer's apprentice. He remained with the Taylor family until adulthood. The Farr family was also very prominent in Ogden.

from the Tabernacle was paying attention to [her]."[17] They were married on April 26, 1911, in the Salt Lake Temple, eventually building a small house on 800 West in Salt Lake City not far from Cannon's childhood home. Two sons soon came along, followed by a daughter.

Part of Cannon's duties as Tabernacle organist included giving public recitals at the Tabernacle several times each week. The uniquely designed Tabernacle with its egg-shaped dome roof and seemingly magical acoustic properties was a popular destination for travelers. A recital series was first instituted in 1900 as an attraction for the steady stream of railroad travelers who passed through Salt Lake City, though the recitals were held somewhat sporadically. Following his appointment as organist in 1901, McClellan lobbied for significant changes to the original pioneer-era Tabernacle organ. The firm of W. W. Kimball completely overhauled the internal workings of the organ, leaving the original casework (and some pipes) intact. The enlarged organ generated considerable excitement and with the addition of Kimball and Cannon to the Tabernacle staff, recitals gradually morphed into a daily event. By 1911, a recital rotation had emerged with each organist playing two recitals per week at 12:10 p.m. Lasting approximately forty-five minutes, the recitals featured popular organ works, arrangements of orchestral and opera movements, as well as an improvisation on a "Mormon hymn tune." Tourists seeking additional information could visit the Bureau of Information located near the south gate on Temple Square; there they could purchase brochures, including one entitled "The Salt Lake Tabernacle and World Famed Organ — Graphic description. Profusely illustrated."

McClellan developed a formula for recital programs which was emulated by both Cannon and Kimball. In a presentation titled "Program Building for the Masses," given at the 1911 convention of National Association of Organists in Ocean Grove, New Jersey, McClellan explained that through trial and error, the Tabernacle organists had learned that the most well-received recitals contained a balance of "old standards" and lighter pieces. "As now given, the programs usually include four numbers—the first a brilliant overture, the second a group

17. "Lettie Taylor Cannon Life History," in Mark Ballstaedt, *A Song of the Heart: The Story of Tracy Y. Cannon* (Heirloom Press, 2000).

of lighter pieces, of which one is always an 'Old Melody'; third, a popular selection, and fourth, another classical organ number."[18]

Cannon's recital repertoire leaned heavily on contemporary pieces of the day, operatic transcriptions, organ sonata movements, and the occasional work by Bach. The recitals tended to be light-hearted and palatable—nothing that would challenge listener sensibilities with excessive chromaticism, nor were the pieces overly taxing to the organist. Cannon favored works by American and Italian composers, as well as his teacher, Guilmant.

In addition to the daily recitals, the organists were also responsible for accompanying the Tabernacle Choir not only for regular rehearsals and local services and performances, but also for tours. The Tabernacle Choir embarked on a tour of the Pacific Northwest in 1909 and a two-month tour of the East Coast in late 1911. Cannon did not travel with the choir; instead he remained in Salt Lake, covering single-handedly for McClellan and Kimball while they were away.

Cannon speculated that it was the Tabernacle organ (personified by McClellan) rather than the Tabernacle Choir which generated the interest of outsiders. "I really think [McClellan] did more to advertise Utah, in bringing fame to Utah, than any person up to his time."[19] Though the 1902 Kimball organ served the Tabernacle well for several years, by 1914 it had begun to deteriorate due to heavy use and Utah's dry climate. Cannon and McClellan petitioned for the organ to be rebuilt, this time by the Austin Organ Company of Hartford, Connecticut. A new console was installed just before the 1915 summer recital season as a stopgap measure that would keep the Kimball organ playable until work could begin on the new components in the fall. The enlarged organ was flanked on either side by new towers, giving the instrument its signature façade. It was playable (though not entirely completed) in time for April general conference in 1916 and was immediately hailed a success.

Following his marriage to Lettie, Cannon continued to divide his time between students in Salt Lake City and Weber Academy

18. Valerie Harris, "How the West Was Won: The Impact of Railroad Tourism on the Development of Pipe Organ Recitals at the Salt Lake Tabernacle" (DMA diss., Arizona State University, 2022), 71.

19. Annie Rosella Compton, "John J. McClellan, Tabernacle Organist" (master's thesis, Brigham Young University, 1951), 45.

in Ogden, teaching harmony and piano to supplement his modest Tabernacle organist salary. Cannon had long been interested in improving musicianship within the church, a vision which was more encompassing than the instruction of individual students and his own performances. In May 1913 he was made music director of the Pioneer Stake, where he and Lettie resided, and formed an association with other local musicians for the purpose of providing support for auxiliary musicians and raising the musical standards of the wards in the stake. The group was called the Pioneer Stake Choristers and Organists Association and Cannon was named its leader. The society listed five objectives: (1) to improve the choir singing and organ playing in all meetings in the wards; (2) to bring the choir leaders and organists in closer touch with each other; (3) to better prepare choristers and organists to more intelligently perform their work; (4) to prepare new choristers and organists; and (5) to promote musical contests and devise other means to increase interest in musical activities connected to church work. The following year Cannon directed the stake's musicians in a performance of Gounod's *Redemption* held in the Assembly Hall on Temple Square with McClellan at the organ. Cannon wrote his first piece of sacred music, a choral setting of "O My Father," for the choirs of the Pioneer Stake.[20] His experience with the association seemed to be quite formative for Cannon, not only reinforcing his conviction that the quality of music within the church could be improved through training, but also allowing him to refine coaching methods.

It was during this period that Cannon began to experiment with more formalized curriculum development. During the summer of 1917, he organized a six-week course for public school music teachers. The course was taught in Cannon's Templeton Building studio in Salt Lake City, though it is unclear how many teachers actually registered. Later that fall Cannon joined the music faculty at the Latter-day Saints University (LDSU) in Salt Lake City.

Utah's system of higher education grew out of a network of academies (essentially high schools) which were sponsored and financially

20. Cannon's setting would prove to be one of his most enduring. It was performed by numerous choirs, including the Mormon Tabernacle Choir. In 1954, the piece was sung by a large youth choir at a 1954 MIA regional conference held at the Hollywood Bowl.

supported by church congregations during the territorial period. Access to public education increased after Utah obtained statehood in 1896, boosted by compulsory school attendance and a secure tax base. To meet ongoing demand for qualified educators, the chief responsibility of the academies shifted from educating youth to training public school teachers, granting two-or-four-year diplomas. The State Board of Education attempted to gain control of the state's many teacher training programs, which issued their own certificates and diplomas with requirements that varied from institution to institution. The board's requirements became increasingly more rigorous, initially focusing only on a candidate's moral character, but eventually expanding to include academic competencies. As a result, the colleges scrambled to adjust their training programs to fit the state's new requirements.[21]

LDSU had struggled from its inception in 1892 to gain footing in this shifting environment. The university occupied a variety of buildings around the city's core before permanent facilities were finally constructed on the northern side of the block east of Temple Square.[22] Though owned by the LDS Church, the curriculum of LDSU did not include religious instruction, nor did it include any sort of theological seminary, as would come to be the expectation for church-owned institutions of higher learning by the mid-twentieth century. Rather, with very little distinction between church and state in early twentieth-century Utah, it was assumed that Mormon theology and doctrine were "baked into" the broader culture.

The university had expanded to include a small music department in 1914, absorbing much of the faculty of the privately owned Utah Conservatory of Music, which McClellan had founded some years earlier.[23] The LDSU School of Music was chaired by B. Cecil

21. Clyde Bartonek, "The History of Teacher Certification in Utah" (master's thesis, University of Utah, 1948), 63.

22. For more information regarding higher education in Utah in the first part of the twentieth century, see Thomas Alexander, *Mormonism in Transition: A History of the Latter-day Saints 1890–1930* (Greg Kofford Books, 2012).

23. It is not entirely clear how connected the Utah Conservatory of Music (founded in 1910) and the Utah School of Music (founded in 1904 by McClellan, Cannon, and others) were. By all accounts, they were separate enterprises but likely involved many of the same music instructors (including McClellan). "Utah School of Music is Organized" and "Theological Arpeggios," *Salt Lake Tribune*, January 1, 1910.

Gates, who served as assistant director of the Tabernacle Choir from 1916 to 1935. Cannon was pleased to be a member of the university's faculty, and felt the new School of Music provided students with an education similar to what he had experienced at the conservatory in Berlin. *The Salt Lake Telegram* reported:

> Americans need not worry about going to Europe to get a musical education because they can get it here in America, is the opinion of Tracy Y. Cannon, assistant organist at the Tabernacle. Mr. Cannon, who studied piano with Alberto Jonás in Berlin and organ with Albert A. Stanley at Ann Arbor, and with Alexander Guilmant in Paris, passed eight years getting instruction from foreign teachers. "We do not need to go there to learn music," said Mr. Cannon. "We have excellent teachers here in America."[24]

24. "U.S. Supersedes Old World as Mecca for All Music Lovers," *Salt Lake Telegram*, September 23, 1917.

CHAPTER FOUR

"SINGING THE SONGS OF ZION"

In 1918, the church's organizational structure underwent significant modification following the appointment of President Heber J. Grant. Sensing a need for administrative reform in view of the church's financial and public relations debacles of the previous two decades, Grant instituted a number of changes, including the addition of general authorities to manage auxiliary boards, regularly scheduled meetings with the church's various administrative groups, and setting in order the church's financial obligations by continuing to divest from the many business interests with which the church was entangled. Grant's presidency ushered in a new era for the church culturally as well. Though Grant had three polygamous wives, only his wife Augusta was still living at the time of his presidency, making him the last church president to practice polygamy as well as the first to observe monogamy. He was also the first church president born in Utah which meant he had no personal connection with the bygone Nauvoo era. A Utah man of business through and through, he was inclined toward innovation and modernization on all fronts. It was during Grant's presidency that the church began to abandon many of its more isolationist tendencies and attempted to find its place in broader American society, a process which would not be fully realized for several more decades.

Among the adjustments Grant made to church administration was the formation of a brand new committee which would dictate LDS music and define its character moving into the modern era. Grant had an extremely personal connection to hymn-singing, frequently citing his own struggle with tone-deafness, which he claimed to have overcome by singing hymns ad nauseam, much to the chagrin of colleagues and acquaintances. Grant recounted this experience not only to illustrate the power of dogged persistence, but also to preach the importance of the "songs of Zion."[1] Grant seemed particularly concerned that sacred music be brought into strict alignment with church doctrine. While serving as a member of the Quorum of the Twelve Apostles, Grant had written an article for *The Improvement Era* entitled "Sing Only What We Believe." In it he expressed utter dismay at the performance of the popular hymn "Just As I Am" at a stake music contest, stating that, "It would be next to impossible to find more false teachings in so short a space than are contained in the above hymn." Grant objected to the hymn's overt declaration that salvation comes by grace alone, as the LDS Church instead embraced a more works-oriented theology. Grant continued, "The more beautiful the music by which false doctrine is sung, the more dangerous it becomes. I appeal to all Latter-day Saints, and especially to our choirs, never to sing the words of a song, no matter how beautiful and inspiring the music may be, where the teachings are not in perfect accord with the truths of the gospel."[2]

To provide adequate guidance for the church's musicians and avoid future theological faux pas, the General Music Committee was organized in 1920; its first meeting was held on September 28 in Gates's LDSU School of Music studio. Following Grant's new administrative protocol, which gave increased authority to the Quorum of the Twelve Apostles in overseeing church affairs, apostle Melvin J. Ballard (himself an amateur musician) was appointed as the committee's chair. The rest of the committee included a representative from each of the church's auxiliary presidencies (important because at this time, the auxiliaries maintained a considerable amount of autonomy in addition to boasting robust musical programs of their own) as well as professional musicians drawn from the Tabernacle staff and the faculty of the LDSU School of Music: Cannon, Gates, Kimball, Evan Stephens, George D. Pyper, McClellan, Anthony Lund, Lizzie Edwards, Margaret Summerhays, Jane Romney

1. Darwin Wolford, *Song of the Righteous* (Cedar Fort, 1995), 115.
2. Heber J. Grant, "Sing Only What We Believe," *Improvement Era*, July 1912.

Crawford, Horace G. Whitney, and Joseph Ballantyne. Whitney died in October 1920, creating a vacancy that was filled by George Careless. Cannon was gratified to be included on the committee in spite of his young age, and he hoped his vision for improved music within the church would soon be realized. Letters were sent to all stake presidencies in the church informing them of the newly organized committee and urging stakes to organize music committees of their own so that they might disseminate any practical knowledge or decision the general committee may dispense.[3]

At their first meeting the committee tackled its most pressing problem: creating a library of choral anthems with relevant, doctrinally sound texts, and the proper "Mormon sound." Choral culture was quite robust within the LDS Church during the 1920s, in contrast to much of the mainline Protestant sector which had adopted professional quartets that either bolstered amateur choirs or replaced them entirely.[4] This was due in part to the prominence of the Mormon Tabernacle Choir, which relied on local congregations to provide "feeder choirs," but was certainly impacted by the church's geographical isolation during its early Utah period, when choir rehearsals and church-sponsored singing schools were important to the development of communal cohesion. Choir directors were eager not only for a repertoire possessing lyrics aligned with Mormon doctrine, but also for anthems by "home composers." It is not clear what exactly led to the preoccupation with "home composers"; though there was certainly objection by church members to choral music that was overly "papist" as well as anything that smelled of English high church tractarianism. Similarly offensive was the overly sensual operatic music which had infiltrated many East Coast protestant churches. More than material musical characteristics, it is likely the church's collective fixation with "homegrown composers" stemmed from the rather insular notion

3. Briefly in 1943–44, the notion of a ward music committee was elevated to "ward music guild." The guild was intended to encompass all musical activities of the ward, including the auxiliary organizations as well as social/recreational music and spoke to an effort at "professionalization" of sacred music. Outlines for guild meetings were published in the *Improvement Era*. Letter to Bishops, September 14, 1944, General Music Committee Files, CHL (hereafter, Music Files).

4. Paul Westermeyer, *Te Deum*, (Fortress Press, 1998).

that music written by LDS composers, and therefore imbued with the "proper spirit of God," was inherently superior to music by non-LDS composers, a belief elucidated by Grant, "The singing of the songs of Zion, though imperfectly, with the inspiration of God, will touch the hearts of the honest more effectively than if sung well without the Spirit of God."[5]

Initial efforts at creating a body of choral anthems by "home composers" had been spearheaded by early members of the Salt Lake Tabernacle's music staff, including Ebenezer Beesley (*Tabernacle Choir Music: Hymns and Anthems*, 1883) and Joseph J. Daynes (*Latter-day Saint Anthems*, Vol. 1, 1897).[6] Stephens also self-published *Five Favorite Anthems* (1910) and later edited and published two volumes of choral anthems under the title *Temple Anthems* in 1913 and 1918 (the collection's title is deceptive, as the selections have no direct correlation to the LDS temple). *Temple Anthems* included anthems by LDS composers as well as "borrowed" favorites, such as "Cast Thy Burden upon the Lord" from Mendelssohn's *Elijah* and adapted anthems with reworked lyrics such as a Kyrie by Italian composer Guiseppe Concone which was translated to "O Lord Most Merciful." *Temple Anthems* was followed by a collection titled *Modern Anthems,* published in 1919 by Gates. A survey of these early anthems indicates they are nearly all in a major key (even those for somber occasions such as Stephens's setting of "Blessed Are the Dead or Funeral Anthem," with text borrowed from the burial rites of the Anglican Book of Common Prayer). The anthems are homorhythmic and favor pleasantly consonant intervals, such as running series of parallel thirds. Therefore, though they are nearly all written in three- or four-part harmony, they are not taxing to the choir nor to the listener. These collections were very well-received and, according to Deseret Book manager Albert Hooper, sold quickly.[7] Gates promoted both his own anthem collection and those of Stephens to the General Music Committee and even suggested the committee purchase the rights so that the books could be self-distributed. The

5. Heber J. Grant, *Improvement Era*, July 1901.

6. A second volume was never completed; however, Daynes issued a second edition in 1916.

7. General Music Committee, "Meeting Minutes" (January 26, 1921), Music Files.

committee ultimately decided against this, opting instead to focus on the publication of new anthems by local composers.[8]

The result was three volumes of *Deseret Anthems*, the first such anthology published by the church itself. Though the earlier self-published anthem books were popular, it is clear the music committee was motivated to issue its own anthem collection, not only to maintain aesthetic and doctrinal oversight, but financial control as well, as the committee was encouraged to cover its own operating costs and limit allocations from the First Presidency. Gates drafted a letter to be sent to all ward choir leaders explaining the committee's intentions as well as the issues they hoped to address:

> The General Music Committee is making definite plans to compile and publish periodically in book form a set of anthems suitable for use by choirs of the Church. The anthems will be of a grade not too difficult to be serviceable in all choirs of the Church and of sufficient variety to meet the needs of the important events of different seasons. The work of publication involves a great amount of careful preparation and will take some time before the first issue is had, but thereafter it is hoped to have the issues recur at some specified definite dates so that our choristers may have a dependable and reliable source of music—a trying need in the past. By this supply of new and interesting music we feel that a great step has been taken to solve the problem of interest among choir members.[9]

In the meantime, choir directors were encouraged to use *Temple Anthems* and *Modern Anthems*, as well as anthems published outside of collections such as Cannon's 1913 setting of "O My Father."[10]

In addition to providing ward choir directors with suitable music for LDS worship services, the music committee also grappled with questions of both the mundane and philosophical. A current events study guide, written for church teenagers, posed the following question for discussion (which is intriguing not only because the question is directed at general church membership and not necessarily music specialists, but also because it demonstrates the committee's grasp of broader issues in sacred music beyond the LDS church's network):

---

8. Committee on Organization to the General Music Committee, December 31, 1920, Music Files.
9. General Music Committee to Ward Choir Leaders, February 16, 1921, Music Files.
10. General Music Committee to Ward Choir Leaders, February 16, 1921, Music Files.

> The committee on Church Music of the United Lutheran Church of America, which recently held its fifth semi-annual convention in Richmond, Virginia, condemns "show pieces" by the choir. The report says, "All the choir's acts must be acts of worship, and should an anthem be sung, it must be chosen with due reference to the day, season or occasion, and be sung in a manner to inspire devotion."
>
> Should the choir be regarded as a group of entertainers? What is the choir's place? What is the value of congregational singing? Is enough care given to fit the choir singing to the service? What may be done to have choirs and congregations sing with spirit and understanding?[11]

Questions of a more material nature included whether choirs should wear some sort of uniform dress on Sundays (e.g., robes) or whether "evening dress" for the female members of the choir might be appropriate in sacrament meetings on special occasions and whether it was appropriate for the choir and congregation to stand while singing hymns (it was determined that everyone should remain seated except during a "rest" hymn in the middle of the meeting). The suggestion that choir members might wear special attire, so commonplace in other denominations, was contrary to some of Mormonism's most enduring attributes—its approachability and commitment to lay leadership. As noted rather pointedly by Grant:

> There seems to be a constant present tendency—it seems indeed to be a sort of epidemic—to provide some sort of vestments or uniform attire for our choirs. Furthermore, there is a tendency to build up certain special services such as "sunrise services," "sunset services," etc. which would be all right for sun worshippers, or perhaps for certain Christian churches, but seem hardly compatible with the simplicity which characterizes the Church.... All of these things are contrary to the spirit and genius of the simplicity of the Gospel.[12]

In the final months of 1920 another subcommittee was formed, tasked with providing training for ward organists and choristers. Under the LDS model, which still embraced the nonconformist tradition of "untrained, unpaid" clergy, as well as support personnel, local leaders were obliged to supply in-house training for the

11. "Current Events: A Study for the MIA Advanced Senior Classes," *Instructor*, February 1927.

12. Heber J. Grant to General Music Committee, May 10, 1944, Music Files.

musicians that served their congregations. Headed by Kimball, the subcommittee recommended that a questionnaire be sent out to all LDS congregations to ascertain which wards had choirs and how regularly the choirs were rehearsing, in addition to the make, model, age, and condition of all pianos and organs (both reed and pipe) owned by each congregation.[13] The subcommittee further recommended that a five-week institute be held in order to instruct ward organists and choristers in the "rudiments of music, including solfeggio (sight reading), conducting, church-music appreciation, and program-making" as well as the "tuning and care of instruments and vocalization, with something special on the use of the child's voice."[14] Organists would receive additional group or private instruction. The institute was to be held in Salt Lake City, where access to a large number of instruments as well as the Tabernacle Choir and daily Tabernacle organ recitals could provide opportunities for visiting organists and choristers to both practice and witness "practical demonstration." The subcommittee suggested mandatory attendance by two people from each stake.

The inaugural chorister and organist institute was set for June 1921 with an estimated enrollment of 150 individuals. Lecture topics included "The Literature of Hymns," "Cooperation of Chorister and Organist," and "What Music is Appropriate in Worship." Courses were taught by the organ and vocal faculty of the LDSU School of Music, who were paid at their regular school rate.

---

13. This anecdote demonstrates the autonomy from the broader church organization that individual congregations maintained over facilities. By the later half of the twentieth century, the LDS Church had moved to a homogenized facilities model which when coupled with advances in electronic organ design, meant that most wards possessed instruments of a similar make and model. The diverse instruments in various chapels in 1920 posed a significant challenge for the committee as they sought to develop training for amateur ward organists.

14. General Music Committee, "Meeting Minutes" (December 1, 1920), Music Files.

CHAPTER FIVE

"MUSICAL MECCA OF THE WEST"

By 1920, the LDSU School of Music had begun to outgrow the campus it shared with the other university departments. Its offices and some of its studios were temporarily relocated to the Beehive House on the southeast side of Temple Square. Cannon recognized the makeshift arrangements were not sustainable and pleaded with the committee to prioritize finding a permanent location. As luck would have it, the church had been negotiating to repurchase the Gardo House, an opulent mansion located on South Temple Street that had originally been constructed by Brigham Young. The mansion had later served as the official residence of church presidents John Taylor and Wilford Woodruff before the church's financial struggles following the Edmunds-Tucker Act caused them to cede control of the mansion to various private interests. The sale of the house was finalized on March 20, 1920, and church leadership announced that the home would be occupied by the LDS School of Music, now an institution that was entirely separate from the LDSU.[1] With over thirty rooms, some spacious enough to hold several grand pianos, as well as an adjacent building that had a small stage, the house was centrally located at the city's center and promised to become a cultural destination.

An article published in *Musical America* lauded the school's creation, writing, "New Conservatory Promises to Make Salt Lake City Musical Mecca of West."[2] The article revealed the school's unique

1. "Music," *Deseret News*, July 17, 1920.

2. Zora Shaw Hoffman, "New Conservatory Promises to Make Salt Lake City Musical Mecca of West," *Musical America*, October 23, 1920.

position as an educational arm of the church, supported neither by government or through private endowments, making its only homologue the Royal School of Church Music:

> Salt Lake, the promoters of the plan point out, has always been a natural musical center. Church organizations have always been promoters of musical activities, and it is to supply trained material for the musical activities of these organizations that the school has been primarily promoted. But now the institution is going to occupy a broader position, and will be the big factor through which the music of the entire intermountain West is to be guided. It will undoubtedly be the largest conservatory of music west of Chicago.... Complete courses are offered in all branches of music, from beginners' grade to the graduate soloist and teacher. The graduating course covers four years of stringent study, but special work in any department is provided and students may enroll at any time. In addition to the courses in instrumental and vocal studies, special stress is placed upon theory and lecture courses. Other courses meeting a long-felt necessity are the supervisors' course for grade and high schools, and a course for choristers and organists functioning in choir and church organizations. Special emphasis is being placed on a Pedagogical Normal course for high school music teachers. Such a course is not to be obtained elsewhere in the West and at the same time is a very great and timely need.

The LDS School of Music only occupied the Gardo House for one year; on February 27, 1921, papers announced that the site of the building had been sold to the Federal Reserve Bank for $115,000.[3] Provisions were made for the church to relocate the house to a new site (Grant even authorized a feasibility study to determine whether the house could be placed on rollers and moved up State Street). This proved unnecessary, however. In the October 1920 general conference of the church, Grant read a letter from Alfred W. and Elizabeth McCune stating their intention to relocate to California and donate their Salt Lake City mansion to the church for use as the president's official residence. In acknowledgment of the church's continued financial troubles, Grant refused the use of the mansion for his private residence and it was announced in the April 1921 general conference that it would become the home of the LDS School of Music instead.

3. "Church Sells Gardo House Property to U.S. Reserve Bank," *Salt Lake Telegram*, February 27, 1921.

Though the McCune mansion was designed as a residence rather than a school, its location one block to the north of Temple Square, along with its handsomely appointed rooms, made it ideal for a music and art conservatory. The mansion was easily able to accommodate fourteen teaching studios, two lecture rooms, a recital hall, two offices, and a ballroom. As part of the LDS School of Music faculty, Cannon gave private piano and organ lessons as well as group lessons (which were more cost-effective for students and provided a European conservatory atmosphere) in addition to teaching harmony courses. His popularity as a teacher was no doubt enhanced by his position as assistant Tabernacle organist.

In addition to accompanying the Tabernacle Choir for weekly rehearsals, Cannon frequently provided music for a variety of meetings, services, and concerts that were held on Temple Square. By 1923 he and Lettie were the busy parents of six children (his seventh and final child would be born in 1926). The family still resided in the house near Cannon Farm on the west side of Salt Lake City. His children recalled that Cannon filled their lot with fruit trees and a large garden which he irrigated with water pumped from the nearby Jordan River. They remembered waiting for their father to arrive home by street car from work in the city's center. Described as a kind and patient man, he enjoyed reading to his children, cooking them breakfast, and getting them off to school in the mornings.[4]

In spite of his bustling family life and demanding professional schedule, Cannon felt he would benefit professionally from organ study, so during the summer of 1923, he left his family at home and traveled to New York City to study under Pietro A. Yon.

Yon immigrated in 1907 from Rome to New York City where he served first as organist at the Church of Saint Francis Xavier in Manhattan and later at Saint Patrick's Cathedral for the remainder of his career. Upon his arrival in the United States, Yon opened a small music studio. His brother Constantine, also an organist and choir director, later joined him and in 1914 they opened a more expansive studio together under the name Yon Music Studios, which was located in the Carnegie Hall Studio Towers directly

4. "Cannon Children Remembrances, 1979," Cannon Papers.

above Carnegie Hall. The studio housed a 6-rank, 3-manual George Kilgen and Sons pipe organ (Opus 4414, 1929).[5]

As a composer, Yon wrote primarily liturgically based works and he was noted in his lifetime as an expert on Catholic chant and liturgy.[6] It is unclear whether Cannon studied any of the composer's own works during his 1923 training; however, Cannon added two works of Yon to his regular Tabernacle recitals in the year following his return to Utah: the *Sonata Romantica* published in 1922, and the popular *Humoresque 'L'Organo Primitivo' (Toccatina for Flute)* from *Twelve Divertimenti,* published in 1915. Additionally, Yon was recognized for his impeccable and virtuosic pedal technique. Cannon recalled that Yon gave him, "the best pedal technique I have ever received." *The Salt Lake Tribune* printed Cannon's assessment of his trip upon his return to Salt Lake at the end of the summer:

> "I am convinced that Utah has as much musical talent as any other community of equal population in the United States," said Tracy Y. Cannon, Salt Lake organist and pianist, on his return Friday afternoon from New York City, where he has been studying this summer.
>
> "But I feel sure," he continued, "that the great majority of our music students do not realize the tremendous amount of technical practice over a period of years that is necessary to give the student an adequate freedom of expression in interpreting the great masterpieces of music. The main difference between the successful musician and the failure is not so much that one has more musical talent than the other, but rather because one is willing to spend years of painstaking work in developing proficiency, while the other thinks his natural musical talent will carry him through. What students need is a longer period of technical training than many of them have any idea of. They must be willing to spend many years in the closest study of details, developing arm, hand and finger dexterity, in phrasing, and other things that are essential to the expression of emotions through music."
>
> ... Mr. Cannon said that he greatly enjoyed his studies in the east and that he has found new teaching material for the piano, as well as many new organ pieces. He heard the great organ in the Wanamaker store at Philadelphia, also the organ in the Eastman theater at Rochester, and, although one is said to be the largest organ in the world and

5. Pipe Organ Database, Organ Historical Society, Organ, ID:59810.
6. "Pietro Yon," *Caecilia* 64, no. 7 (1937).

the other the last word in mechanical perfection and tonal variety, still he is of the opinion that the Salt Lake tabernacle organ is unsurpassed by any in tonal beauty.[7]

The year 1923 also began a period of intense change for the Tabernacle organ staff. In November, McClellan embarked on a long Pacific coast recital tour. While performing at the San Francisco civic auditorium, he suffered a nervous breakdown (by some accounts a stroke).[8] McClellan was forced to cancel the remaining twenty-two engagements on his tour, and he and his wife remained on the coast so McClellan could recuperate at a sanitarium.

McClellan was put on extended leave which was extremely taxing on Cannon and Kimball as they shouldered McClellan's Tabernacle duties as well as his teaching load. At the April 1924 general conference, Cannon and Kimball were each promoted to the position of organist and Alexander Schreiner was hired as assistant organist.[9] Organist Frank W. Asper joined the staff two weeks after Schreiner. McClellan, having sufficiently recovered from his breakdown, returned to Salt Lake City just as Schreiner was preparing to leave for advanced study in Paris. Schreiner requested that church leadership allow him a two year leave of absence, which they reluctantly granted.[10] The daily organ recital series at the Tabernacle continued to grow, expanding for the first time to a year-round series in January 1925. Unfortunately, McClellan's health continued to decline and in July 1925, he suffered a series of strokes before passing away a few weeks later on August 2.[11]

7. Tracy Cannon Praises Utah's Musical Talent," *Salt Lake Tribune*, September 2, 1923.

8. "McClellan Suffers Nervous Breakdown," *Diapason*, January 15, 1924, 9.

9. Daniel Frederick Berghout, "Alexander Schreiner: Mormon Tabernacle Organist" (PhD diss., Brigham Young University, 2001).

10. Berghout, "Mormon Tabernacle Organist," 16.

11. An apocryphal tale in *The Diapason* (September 1925) says that McClellan first collapsed onto the keys on July 3 just as he was completing his final noon recital. "The last number on his program was Handel's Largo and as he was playing it suddenly both of his hands fell on to the keys."

CHAPTER SIX

"MUSIC IS NO LONGER FOR THE FEW, BUT FOR ALL"

In 1924, the LDS School of Music experienced two significant changes; Grant announced that following the death of Elizabeth McCune, the school would be renamed the McCune School of Music and Art in her honor.[1] Though perhaps not intentional, this represented another shift in the school's public-facing image; a name that did not directly indicate the church's involvement in the institution was useful as the school began to place itself on the national stage. The following year, Gates announced his resignation as director, having received an offer to chair the music department of Utah State Agricultural College (later renamed Utah State University) in Logan, Utah.[2]

Following Gates's resignation, Cannon was appointed director of the McCune School by church leadership. Cannon was an apt choice, not only given his long involvement with the inner workings of the church's music program as well as his reputation as a pedagogue, but also his propensity for leadership and educational development within the community. Speaking before a meeting of the Salt Lake City Kiwanis Club in 1924 following his promotion, Cannon said: "The abundance of music is proof it satisfies a human need and is essential for complete living. Music has a universal appeal and is no longer for the few, but for all. Its educational and cultural value is recognized."[3]

1. Heber J. Grant, *Conference Report,* April 4, 1924.

2. Gates remained on the teaching faculty of the McCune School from 1924 until 1932, dividing his time between the two institutions.

3. "Kiwanis is Told Music Needed for Full Life," *Salt Lake Telegram,* May 3, 1924.

Cannon articulated his goals for the McCune School even more clearly than Gates had. The 1925 enrollment brochure eloquently states:

> The McCune School of Music and Art is an institution, organized and conducted to disseminate education in music and allied arts, both in theory and practice, from the beginning steps to mature attainment. Its aim is to encourage the serious and fundamental study of music, and to establish such ideals, and to provide such courses as will ensure its students becoming alike proficient in performance, sound in knowledge, and ethical in conduct. It lays emphasis upon the desirability of acquiring theoretical training concurrently with technical development, and upon the necessity of such training if the music education is to be worthy of the name; at the same time it offers unexcelled facilities for pursuance and consummation of such theory training, both in personnel and equipment.[4]

Embedded in Cannon's aims for the school is reference to its rather unique, community-oriented mission. Unlike many music conservatories, which had as their primary objective the production of music professionals and the training of prodigies, the McCune School was intended to serve the broader interests of the population at large, providing music training to amateurs as well as aspiring professionals. The majority of the school's students fell into the former category; despite Cannon's best efforts to make McCune competitive with other schools of music, only 121 students ever obtained degrees.[5]

One of Cannon's first actions as director was to obtain accreditation for the school. Cannon recognized that in order to compete on the national stage, his music conservatory would need recognition from a governing body outside the state of Utah.[6] The National

4. Tracy Cannon, *Enrollment Brochure 1925–1926*, McCune School of Music and Art Files (hereafter, McCune files).

5. Donald G. Schaefer, "Contributions of the McCune School of Music and Art to Music Education in Utah, 1917–1957" (master's thesis, Brigham Young University, 1962), 36.

6. While the State Board of Education continued to recognize public school music teacher diplomas from McCune until 1930, these diplomas were increasingly invalid outside of the state, where a Bachelor of Arts or Science had become the gold standard for obtaining teacher licensure. A study published by the United States Bureau of Education indicated that many so-called "schools of music" were "not much beyond the rudimentary stages of organization … and do not require anything from students except regular attendance and prompt payment of bills." For this reason, licensing bodies had grown wary of diplomas or certificates from unrecognized institutions and began

Association of Schools of Music (NASM) was organized in 1924 as a group of music schools (representing both colleges and universities as well as independent music conservatories) providing higher education programs for music and music-adjacent disciplines. Cannon was elected to the group as an individual member in 1926, and almost immediately began seeking admission for the McCune School. In 1927, the school instituted a Bachelor of Music degree, the curriculum of which was approved by NASM.[7] The school still continued to offer less rigorous artist diplomas; however, the entire institution was converted to a quarter credit-hour system in order to comply with NASM requirements. Despite this adjustment, the University of Utah refused to recognize transfer credit from the McCune School; however, the university's president, George Thomas, confided in Cannon that the school's new bachelor's degree (along with the potential for the school's incorporation) would go a long way in allaying the university's concern over McCune's potential transience.[8] Ultimately, the McCune School was granted full accreditation by NASM in December 1928:[9] "The McCune School has achieved real distinction in being accepted by the National Association as only those schools whose courses, faculty and scholarship measure up to the high standards adopted by the association may be admitted.... Thus far, only thirty eight of the six hundred schools of music in America have been admitted to institutional membership."[10]

Cannon was determined that the McCune School's institutional reputation be consistent with other music conservatories in the eastern United States; he was also mindful of the financial constraints

requiring a bachelor's degree. Waldo S. Pratt, "Instruction in Music, Biennial Survey of Education, Part 1 (Washington, DC: Bureau of Education, 1921), 257–68.

7. Tracy Cannon to students and faculty, August 27, 1927, McCune files.

8. The McCune School was never incorporated. See Salt Lake County Incorporation Index and Incorporation Files Index Salt Lake County, and Tracy Cannon to Sylvester Q. Cannon, July 22, 1927, McCune files.

9. Prior to 1928, NASM did not grant institutional membership, only membership for individuals. During the four-year period between its founding in 1924 and 1928, NASM developed minimum standards that institutions must meet in order to be admitted. In order to become a charter member institution, the school applied and was then investigated in person by a member of the executive committee (Kenneth M. Bradley in the case of McCune). See Carl Neumeyer, "A History of the National Association of Schools of Music" (PhD diss., Indiana University, 1954).

10. "Now in Association," *Salt Lake Telegram,* December 9, 1928.

inherent in maintaining a privately funded educational institution, particularly with pressure from church authorities to make the McCune School a profitable venture and was therefore curious about the management of other music schools. As such, while attending the 1928 NASM annual meeting in Chicago, he interviewed the directors of several institutions, including the Chicago Music College, Bush Conservatory of Music, and the Sherwood Music School.

Cannon persisted in his quest for recognition of McCune School credits by the University of Utah without success. The university's registrar cited many reasons over the years, including the university's practice of not accepting credit from independent music conservatories and McCune's lack of accreditation by the Northwest Association of Secondary Schools and Colleges.[11] Other local institutions such as Brigham Young University and Utah State Agricultural College accepted McCune's credit unequivocally, leaving Cannon frustrated by the University of Utah's lack of cooperation. Ultimately, McCune's singular focus on music prevented it from competing with the local universities that offered students diverse coursework and a more "traditionally" well-rounded education. In fact, many students attended the McCune School only for private music instruction, completing general studies at the University of Utah or BYU.

The church initially intended the McCune School to be self-sustaining, aside from the use of church property, and to function solely on money derived from student tuition. This was simply not feasible, at least not in light of Cannon's objective of keeping costs affordable and within reach of middle-class students. To this end, Cannon experimented with a number of creative solutions to generate increased enrollments (and therefore revenue), including providing courses for children and non-matriculating adults. A preparatory division was added during the 1925–1926 school year, "in order to provide children with proper instruction in music, dancing, and dramatic art."[12] One novel approach introduced into the preparatory division was group instruction of piano and violin to classes consisting of twelve or more children at one time. Classes were held weekly during the

11. Ronald B. Thompson to Tracy Cannon, August 10, 1943, and Tracy Cannon to Charles E. Skidmore, undated, McCune files.

12. Tracy Y. Cannon, *Report of the 1925–1926 School Year*, McCune files.

school year and two times per week during a special six-week course convened during summer recess. To complete the program fully required eight terms, at which point the student could continue on to private study with the school's faculty. Group piano instruction for children was so successful that satellite campuses were eventually opened in the Sugarhouse area (a suburb southeast of Salt Lake City) as well as in Ogden, Bountiful, South Salt Lake City, and Spanish Fork.[13] Few buildings could accommodate twelve or more pianos in a single room, so children completed their piano lessons on keyboards that were drawn to scale on paper.

The campus group piano model was later expanded to include a "neighborhood way of teaching piano"; under this framework, McCune's piano teachers were dispatched into the various neighborhoods that surrounded Salt Lake City to teach lessons twice each week in homes, thereby saving parents a trip into the city for lessons. These courses were advertised at the low rate of six dollars per month. To generate interest in the new program, Cannon gave lesson demonstrations in local chapels.

Beginning in the summer of 1926, the McCune School began to offer additional summer school courses for children. These sessions lasted either three or six weeks and provided instruction in music, dramatic art, and dancing complete with weekly "twilight recitals" held on the school's expansive lawn.[14] For a time, the school's unfinished attic was converted into art studio space where children's drawing and watercolor classes were held.

A permanent summer orchestra and band program was eventually added under the direction of Albert Shepherd, Reginald Beales, and William Lym in 1928. Additionally in the summer of 1928, the McCune School joined forces with LDS College and the Deseret Gymnasium to host a six-week summer camp for youth. Swimming classes were scheduled daily at the gymnasium, in addition to open plunges with times reserved exclusively for girls. For boys, shop training was offered at the LDS College including instruction in, "cabinet work, lathe turning, construction of useful articles for

13. The Sugarhouse preparatory school was located at 2032 South 1100 East, Salt Lake City.

14. Tracy Y. Cannon, *Report of the 1925–1926 School Year*, McCune files.

the home, furniture repairing, making over old furniture, upholstery, finishing, and polishing." Boys wishing for an "office-work" experience could elect to take penmanship or typing. In addition to band and orchestra instruction, students could take group vocal and piano lessons, ear training, and private instruction from McCune faculty.

After 1927 the school's budget was controlled by the presiding bishopric of the church, headed by Sylvester Q. Cannon (yet another son of George Q. Cannon). In 1928, Cannon wrote a letter to Bishop Cannon stating that, "It has been clearly demonstrated that it is impossible to make a profit on the teaching of advanced pupils in this school," and suggesting that the school might become more profitable if it offered additional year-round instruction for children in areas beside music.[15] As Cannon remained committed to keeping the school's tuition low, his only options for increasing revenue were to bring in more students or increase the percentage of tuition fees the school retained before paying its teachers. McCune received appropriations from the presiding bishopric throughout the 1920s to help offset its operating expenses; however, a new presiding bishopric was less supportive and balked at McCune's need for continued financial support. In response Cannon wrote, "The fine arts, in their higher expression, have never yet been able to flourish on a commercial basis but have always had to receive financial assistance. I have many times hoped that this might be the attitude toward this school, rather than that it must be made a commercial success."[16]

In order to cobble together a living wage, many McCune faculty members were also employed by other institutions such as BYU and the University of Utah. There was significant crossover between the organ and vocal departments and the Salt Lake Tabernacle's music staff; members of the Tabernacle organ staff were primarily responsible for all organ instruction at McCune, while McCune's vocal department included a number of former and future Tabernacle Choir directors such as Gates, Lund, and Richard P. Condie. Other instructors taught in multiple departments at McCune, such as theory and piano, thereby increasing their workload and compensation. McCune's piano department was consistently its largest

15. Tracy Y. Cannon to Sylvester Cannon, May 24, 1928, McCune files.
16. Tracy Y. Cannon to Joseph L. Wirthlin, July 27, 1942, McCune files.

with over fifty instructors at its peak. Cannon was the only faculty member to be classified as full-time; he was paid a modest director's salary in addition to receiving payment for his teaching load. The school also had a small support staff which included several secretaries as well as an on-site groundskeeper who at one point resided in the school's basement.

McCune's core curriculum consisted of harmony, musicianship, conducting, and music history and appreciation, which was supplemented by individual instruction as well as small and large ensembles. Following its institutional admission into NASM in 1928, Cannon reorganized the theory department to include advanced harmony and counterpoint, with parallel musicianship courses that covered ear training, dictation, sight singing, and keyboard skills. Students seeking a four-year music degree were required to complete fifty-one quarter hours of theory (which increased to seventy-five quarter hours after 1932).[17] The two-year artist and teacher diplomas were less rigorous, requiring minimal theory coursework. Students pursuing the teacher diploma were required to teach gratis for two hours per week for one academic year, mostly in the school's preparatory division.

Cannon was adamant about the inclusion of ensembles, both large and small, in the McCune School's offerings arguing that these not only furnished musicians for both church and civic events but also provided young people with the "proper" sort of amusement. In a letter to public school music teachers rife with sensationalism (not to mention undercurrents of racism), Cannon wrote:

> You have often heard it said that the spirit of jazz is rampant in the land, that our youth are pleasure-mad and seeking more the riches of the earth than the riches of the spirit. You are one who has set his hand to the task of stemming the tide of crass materialism.... You can help us build enrollment of earnest students by speaking a good word for us when the occasion arises. And you will be richly compensated by the influence for good these thoroughly trained students will bring back to their community.[18]

---

17. In addition to music courses, bachelor's degree candidates were required to take non-music elective courses from the University of Utah. These included English, psychology, education, history, philosophy, and French or German. McCune School of Music and Art, Announcements, 1926–1927, McCune files.

18. Tracy Cannon to teachers, August 28, 1928, McCune files.

The McCune Symphony Orchestra, initially under the direction of Gates, was later overseen by Asper who continued to direct it for twenty-five years. Orchestra rehearsals and performances were held in various locations over the years including Barratt Hall on the campus of LDS College, the Assembly Hall, and the McCune recital hall. Under Asper's direction, a second group was formed for beginning and intermediate musicians which fed into the McCune Symphony Orchestra. High school students from surrounding institutions were permitted to play in both the beginning and symphony orchestras, a critical community outreach as not all high schools offered orchestra classes at the time. Orchestra members paid a modest fee of $5 to participate each season with additional expenses covered by donations. As a gesture of public outreach, concert tickets were mailed to public schools in the surrounding area so that students in grades nine through twelve could attend.

Undoubtedly inspired by his time in Europe, where he witnessed a performance of Bach's "Passion Music" in St. Paul's Cathedral, Cannon organized the Bach Chorus in 1927 to "render publicly the works of J. S. Bach and other vocal compositions of highest musical value that are not heard in this community." The choir's inaugural concert included a performance of Bach's cantata, *Du Hirte Israel, höre*, BWV 104, sung in English. While Bach works were a staple of the choir's repertoire, they also sang other masterworks of the late Renaissance and Baroque eras including works by Palestrina and Handel. The choir was open to McCune students, but was also intended as a public outreach. Cannon sent recruitment letters to members of the community known to be strong singers and have an interest in choral masterworks.

Despite his demanding administrative schedule, Cannon remained heavily involved in the school's theory department, teaching harmony, counterpoint, and composition. A student recalled that Cannon taught his theory classes in his office (which was by then located in the mirrored, pink, silk-walled room on the first floor adjacent to the recital hall). His texts of choice included treatises such as Ferruccio Busoni's *Sketch of a New Aesthetic of Music* (1911) and Arnold Schoenberg's *Harmonielehre* (1922), which Cannon had received from Alexander Schreiner who was teaching from Schoenberg's text at UCLA.[19] Cannon inaugurated a series of weekly student recitals, held on Thursday afternoons in the school's recital hall, to provide students with much-needed performance opportunities. His children recalled that Cannon seldom missed a student recital, and as they grew older, they would often attend with him.[20]

19. An English translation of Schoenberg's text was not published until 1978. While at UCLA, Schreiner, a native German speaker, was called upon to use his language skills to teach beginning harmony courses using Schoenberg's book. Grant Johannesen recalled first seeing the Schoenberg text in Cannon's harmony course at McCune but makes no reference to it being written in German. Grant Johannesen, *Journey of An American Pianist* (University of Utah Press, 2006), 13; and Alexander Schreiner, *Alexander Schreiner Reminisces* (Publisher's Press, 1984), 56.

20. "Cannon Children Remembrances, 1979," Cannon Papers.

CHAPTER SEVEN

"YOU'LL SING BETTER AND MORE HAPPILY FROM THIS BOOK"

In addition to providing congregations with a "suitably Mormon" anthology of choral anthems, the General Music Committee also recognized the immediate need for an updated body of hymnody. In 1920, at the time of the committee's formation, LDS congregations had a number of hymnals at their disposal, yet none was used universally. The first of these, *Latter-day Saints' Psalmody: A Collection of Original Tunes*, was first published in 1889 and was the brainchild of Salt Lake Tabernacle staff, including Stephens, Beesley, Daynes, Careless, and T. C. Griggs. *Psalmody* was intentionally idiosyncratic; when isolated by both geography and theology, the Mormon response was to create a body of hymns defined by descriptions of mountainous scenery, fiery millennial zeal, and references to the church's health code, the "Word of Wisdom," with scant mention of more traditional Christian subjects such as the crucifixion or adherence to the Christian liturgical calendar. These themes were moderated as the church became more mainstream during the twentieth century, which is evident in later hymnals. Writing in 1915 about contemporary LDS hymnody, Louis Benson, a Presbyterian minister and scholar observed:

> The Mormon hymn book is an exception to the rule of dulness governing sectarian hymnody. Its interest is not in the familiar hymns of worship or of experience, though these take a new color from their surroundings. The interest of Mormon Hymnody is its intense sectarianism. The Mormon history reads like a romance rather than a reality; and the hymn book presents almost every phase and important event of that history as

embedded in contemporaneous hymns or songs that are at worst human documents and that often rise to the level of effective song.[1]

Despite providing a unique collection of "homegrown" LDS hymnody, *Psalmody* never achieved the ubiquity of later twentieth-century hymnals. Its four-part harmony was written in a peculiar (and cumbersome) three-stave engraving format which placed the tenor voice on the top staff rather than the soprano as is more typical.[2] In addition, the hymns in *Psalmody* lacked titles altogether and were instead divided into categories (e.g. sacrament hymns), then printed alphabetically by tune name. Each hymn listed a cross-reference to its original page number to the text-only 1840 Manchester hymnal, which most congregations still used. By the early 1900s, more than ten hymnals were still circulating in congregations and homes throughout the church. Auxiliary organizations such as the Primary and Sunday School also published their own hymn collections, further diluting attempts to create a cohesive Mormon hymnic voice. These included the *Tabernacle Choir Hymnal* (1883), *Sunday School Music Book* (1884), *Deseret Sunday School Song Book* (1892; 1909), *Primary Song Book* (1905), and *Songs of Zion* (1908), which was published primarily for use outside of Utah.

A subcommittee was formed in 1921 to guide an extensive revision of *Psalmody;* however, it was quickly evident that the mammoth task of rewriting the hymnal would require the efforts of the entire committee. Revision work was painfully slow and governed by bureaucratic complexities. Referring to the practice of voting by the show of hands at committee meetings, Stephens wrote in a letter to a friend, "Sometimes we discover impossible barriers to some grand scheme almost before our hands are down, and lucky we are to make

1. Louis F. Benson, *The English Hymn: Its Development and Uses* (John Knox Press, 1915/1962), 432.

2. The precedent for this printing style is difficult to ascertain. It was not a style used in any other LDS hymnal, nor in hymnals that were contemporary to *Psalmody.* It bears some resemblance to the format used in *Sacred Harp* (1844) and *Southern Harmony* (1847), two shape-note hymnals which place the tenor voice on the top staff. It is likely that *Psalmody's* editorial committee was acquainted with these hymnals; however, it is unclear whether they influenced the committee's decision to forgo the more typical SATB engraving style. See Library of Congress, digital collections.

the discovery before too much mischief is done."[3] Stephens also wrote of an apparent rift between the older members of the committee and its more youthful members such as Cannon who, according to Stephens, had yet "to prove they can write hymn tunes."[4]

By early 1923 the *Psalmody* revision committee had completed its survey of the existing publication to determine which hymns would be eliminated. The committee also decided to transcribe all of *Psalmody's* three-stave settings to two staves (a task which was entrusted to Stephens) and to include the entire hymn text (rather than the first few verses), thereby eliminating the need for supplementary text-only hymnals and giving the collection a modern and more user-friendly format that emulated the popular *Songs of Zion*.[5] The resulting hymnal would appeal to the full spectrum of church-goers, not just the musical elite, and provide singable, doctrinally sound hymns that would become the musical voice of the church.

As Stephens went to work transferring the hymns to two staves, other committee members were given the tedious task of sifting through previous hymnal editions to note any changes that had been made from printing to printing. In order to find new hymn texts and tunes, Stephens was charged with surveying back issues of church periodicals for poetry that might be usable as hymn texts.[6] The majority of new texts (particularly those set by Stephens) came from the poetic writings of church apostle Orson F. Whitney. A prolific (though controversial) writer, speaker, and poet, Whitney published a collection of poetry entitled *Voices from the Mountains* in 1922 while serving as a mission president in Liverpool. Altogether,

---

3. Ray L. Bergman, "Letter to Samuel B. Mitton, July 20, 1924," *The Children Sang: The Life and Music of Evan Stephens* (Northwest Publishing, 1992), 241.

4. Bergman, "Letter to Samuel B. Mitton," 241.

5. Stephens was compensated for this task at a rate of $1 per hymn. The other committee members (such as Cannon and Kimball) were not paid for their editorial work; it is likely that Stephens received compensation in part because the work of transcribing the hymns was substantial, but also because Stephens owed $600 (plus 8% interest) to the committee, which he had borrowed to finance a less-than-successful production of his oratorio *The Martyrs* in 1921. The committee agreed to apply part of Stephen's earnings to the $175 in interest that had accrued on his debts. Church Music Committee, "Meeting minutes" (October 19, 1925), Music Files; and Bergman, "Letter to Samuel B. Mitton, 236.

6. General Music Committee, "Meeting Minutes" (March 20, 1924), Music Files.

twenty-three Whitney texts were used in the new hymnal, the majority being stanzas pulled from *Voices*.

Additionally, a blind contest was announced offering a prize of "twenty-five dollars for the best original short closing hymn suitable for choir and congregational singing in the Latter-day Saint meetings" (in this case, hymn refers to both the text and the accompanying music).[7] A contest was also held for the best original sacrament hymn.

Cannon complained that the hymn submissions were "not entirely satisfactory"; however, one prize-winner, Leroy Robertson, caught the attention of the judges. From the small town of Fountain Green in central Utah, Robertson had first made his mark as a violinist in his home town before pursuing composition studies at the New England Conservatory, later returning to central Utah as a public school orchestra teacher. Submitted under the title "Parting," Robertson's winning entry was published as "Most Holy Spirit, We Ask Thee Ere We Part."[8] Robertson was paid $25. The judges (Cannon, Kimball, and Stephens) had never heard of Robertson prior to the contest and Cannon later recalled noting that, "whoever wrote that hymn [Parting] has unusual talent."[9] Stephens was more measured in his assessment of Robertson in a way that is both incisive and prescient:

> At periods [Robertson] is splendidly interesting, then again he suddenly collapses into momentous forced effects that seem quite impracticable, like a person furnishing [a] house, placing a plush article in the kitchen or an old kitchen table near a $1000 piano in the parlour. But he really is fine in major moments and the bigger the work I believe the better the workmanship. His hymn tunes are either lacking interest or over ordained with key changes in the harmonizing. Yet I feel to say watch out for something really good from him.[10]

Second prize was awarded to Stephens (which calls into question the impartiality of the contest). In total, Deseret Book Company was

7. "Prize for Best Closing Song," *Deseret News*, February 11, 1922.

8. General Music Committee, "Meeting Minutes" (September 7, 1922), Music Files.

9. Tracy Cannon, Address given at Brigham Young University, November 25, 1947, Music Files.

10. Bergman, "Letter to Samuel B. Mitton, 242.

billed for 115 new hymns at a rate of $5 each.[11] Though a number of poems and arrangements were sent to the Music Committee from "civilian" church members independent of the contest, these were mostly discarded and the bulk of the hymnal's new selections were composed by members of the committee and their close associates.

In 1927, the General Music Committee released its new hymnal under the title *Latter-day Saint Hymns*, as it had been determined two years prior that the book had undergone such extensive revision that it no longer resembled the 1889 *Psalmody* in any measurable way and therefore required a name all its own. Copies of the hymnal were sold at Deseret Book for $1.00 each, or $11.00 for one dozen.[12] An advertisement proclaimed, "The new book for our choirs and congregations is now ready. It contains 419 songs with music. Many of the old favorites and a lot of new ones. You'll sing better and more happily out of this new book."[13]

Ultimately the 1927 *Latter-day Saint Hymns* represented a significant step forward in the development of LDS hymnody. Though a number of the new hymns lacked durability, the hymnal was accessible in a way that aligned with contemporary publication practices and set a precedent for future LDS hymnals.

---

11. General Music Committee, "Meeting Minutes" (October 19, 1925), Music Files.
12. *Conference Report*, April 1927.
13. *Conference Report*, April 1927.

CHAPTER EIGHT

"TAXING ME TO THE LIMIT"

Cannon's many professional and personal duties began to take a toll on his physical and mental health. In addition to his paid work, Cannon also served on the LDS Church's General Sunday School Board which occupied many of his evening and weekend hours. Additionally, the Tabernacle Choir had recently begun a regular radio broadcast series, which put considerable strain on Cannon and Kimball. The success of the radio station generated interest in increased sacred music programming. Earl Glade, the station's director, pitched a concept called the "KSL Midnight Hour - Sunday Evening on Temple Square" which would incorporate a recital pre-recorded at the Tabernacle and then broadcast late at night so as to capture the West Coast audience. Other programs included "popular operas" transcribed for organ and a program called "The Church of the Air." Cannon was eventually made a music consultant for KSL, responsible for coordinating and advising all church music programming.[1]

By the summer of 1929, Cannon began to feel as though his professional and personal obligations were careening out of control. Perhaps in an attempt to marshal his many diverse duties into some semblance of order, he wrote a detailed outline of his work during the summer of 1929:

> First of all, as Tabernacle organist, I spend three hours practicing daily in preparation. I also play the organ for two regular and various special Tabernacle organ recitals each week. Additionally, I play for one

1. KSL Radio Files, CHL.

> regular and other special Tabernacle Choir practices each week. I also perform one national broadcast each week and perform at the weekly Sunday services at the Tabernacle. My responsibilities with the KSL Radio Sunday evening broadcast include a rehearsal each week and a performance on Sunday evening at the station. I also select the music to be used on the program.[2]

Cannon's professional schedule only intensified as the academic year resumed. He recalled:

> I was away every night at work except two from January to June [1930]. The first night I was home in June, Lettie lined up all the children in front of me and said to them, "We have a very fine man with us tonight and I would like all of you to meet him." She then introduced each of them to me, as follows: "Taylor, this is Tracy Y. Cannon. He is your father." She introduced each one in the same manner and had them all shake hands with me as they said, "I am pleased to meet you, Father." We all had a good laugh.[3]

The demands on Cannon came to a head in the spring of 1930. As the church approached the centennial of its organization in 1830, it was increasingly interested in boosting its public image, calling the previous 100 years, "A Century of Progress."

To celebrate its centennial, the church announced a massive pageant entitled *The Message of the Ages.* Beginning on April 6, 1930, in conjunction with the general conference of the church, the pageant consisted of nightly performances in the Tabernacle spanning two weeks. The *Deseret News* described the pageant as "historic," showing "every epoch since time's dawn."[4]

The Message of the Ages was equal parts spectacle, history, and evangelism, drawing heavily on Mormon scripture and doctrinal teaching (with a strong dose of poetic license) to distill the entirety of human history into a three-act drama told through a Mormon lens. The pageant showcased the work of poet Bertha A. Kleinman, a temple recorder from Mesa, Arizona, as well as scripture passages from the LDS canon. Music for the pageant was selected

2. Cannon, Papers.
3. Cannon Papers.
4. "Pageant Takes Gospel History Through Ages," *Deseret News,* April 5, 1930.

by a committee consisting of Cannon, Lund, Pyper, and Robertson. They chose movements from the wider repertoire such as Haydn's *The Creation*, Handel's *Messiah*, and Mendelssohn's *St. Paul*, as well as oratorios and anthems by local composers such as B. Cecil Gates and Arthur Shepherd. Orchestral transitions that helped facilitate scenery changes were written by Robertson. A number of revered LDS hymns were used in the production, including "Praise to the Man," "See the Mighty Angel Flying," and "Come, Come Ye Saints," which Kleinman referred to as "the Marseillaise of the Latter Days," an allusion to the rallying song of the French Revolution.

Volunteer performers were recruited from wards and stakes within the Salt Lake Valley and beyond—a total of 1,000 actors, singers, and readers according to the *Deseret News*.[5] In addition to performing talent, many volunteered their services behind the scenes sewing costumes (which were purportedly based on "historical models"), creating scenery, and acting as ushers. Choruses and solos were sung by the Salt Lake Tabernacle choir, accompanied by the organ as well as a volunteer 40-piece orchestra directed by Asper.

The Tabernacle itself was transformed into a theater, complete with stage curtains and raised platforms to provide the audience with the best possible view of the actors. In a letter to Kimball (who had taken a leave of absence to serve as president of the Austria-Germany Mission), Cannon wrote: "A huge platform will be built covering the stand the entire choir loft extending from the seventies stand in tiers up to the foot of the pipes on the organ and from the north gallery to the south gallery. In addition to the large curtain used for broadcasting purposes, two other thin curtains will be hung. The organ console will be moved down on to the main floor in front of the speakers stand. The choir will also be seated just in front of the stand on the main floor, as will the orchestra."[6]

The production was a massive undertaking, even for a church accustomed to mounting oratorios and pageants. The planning committee began meeting in January 1930 to discuss logistics, select musical numbers, and find talent. In addition to serving on the committee, Cannon also provided the organ accompaniment for the

5. "Pageant Takes Gospel History Through Ages."
6. Cannon Papers.

entirety of the pageant, as the other three Tabernacle organists were otherwise occupied—Kimball was in Germany, Asper directed the pageant orchestra, and Schreiner was recuperating from influenza in California.[7] In addition to his pageant duties, Cannon continued to accompany the Tabernacle choir in their weekly broadcasts, play three 45-minute organ recitals each week, provide music for general conference, and continue his duties as the McCune School director. In a letter to Kimball, Cannon described his demanding schedule:

> I will probably be ready for a stretcher after the last performance. At least, I will be ready for a rest ... Broadcasts continue each week. Frank [Asper] and I alternate with the solos and I do all the choir accompanying.... I must confess that the work I am doing is taxing me to the limit. With only two organists and with the amount of work the choir is doing, as well as playing three recitals a week, in addition to choir practices and the Sunday service, there is ample work for any man without doing another thing. But, I am trying to keep the school going in addition ... There is much mental anxiety connected with the school work. I see no solution, however, to my difficulties and must hope that strength will be given me to "carry on" until release comes.[8]

Following the pageant, in a letter dated May 7, 1930, Cannon submitted his resignation as Tabernacle organist to President Grant with the request that he be released from his duties by the end of the month, citing the continued physical strain of serving on the Tabernacle staff in addition to his role at the McCune School of Music. Cannon expressed, "much sorrow in leaving the Tabernacle organ where I have played for over twenty years." Cannon also requested a two-month leave of absence from the McCune School so that he might "go east for study," as he felt his pedagogical skills were in need of refinement.[9] Cannon confessed to Kimball that he and Lettie had been contemplating his Tabernacle retirement for a number of months but felt it prudent to wait until after the Centennial Pageant had ended. Cannon shared candidly that he felt the First Presidency had rather eagerly anticipated his resignation. Cannon's retirement would allow them to offer Schreiner the position of

7. Berghout, "Mormon Tabernacle Organist," 53.
8. Tracy Cannon to Edward Kimball, February 19, 1930, Cannon Papers.
9. Tracy Cannon to Edward Kimball, May 13, 1930, Cannon Papers.

"chief organist," a post Schreiner had actively solicited in 1926, and entice him back to Salt Lake City full-time.[10] Cannon wrote:

> President Grant, himself, brought the matter [of retirement] to a head by telling me the other day that he wanted me to devote my time to school, and also, not incidentally, I think they wanted to bring Alec [Schreiner] back. He was to lavish in his praise of Alec that I felt quite sure that the months of constant propaganda by the Nibleys[11] particularly as well as the Lymans[12] have accomplished what has finally taken place.

Cannon seemed to take some solace in his retirement, writing:

> I shall not attempt to keep with my organ practice to any great extent, but I hope that I can devote some time to the piano, at least enough to play for my friends in a social way occasionally. I am sure that being relieved from the nerve wracking work at the Tabernacle, that my nervous conditions improve. I shall have some time to get out in my yard in the mornings and take some exercise and I feel quite happy all in all, although you can well imagine it is exceedingly difficult to leave that wonderful organ.[13]

Cannon's son Ralph recalled that the family—Lettie and the seven children—gathered in the Tabernacle for a private recital at the close of Cannon's tenure, writing, "We all shed tears, both for the occasion of his release as organist and for the quality of the music itself."[14]

Following his retirement from the Tabernacle, Cannon played the organ only sporadically, his time being largely consumed by his duties at the McCune School. Unlike McClellan and Schreiner who toured

---

10. In a letter to the First Presidency dated July 14, 1926, Schreiner requested that he be allowed to fill the vacancy left by McClellan's death by virtue of his training, experience, and talent. Feeling that such a promotion would be unfair to Cannon who had seniority and Asper who had maintained more regular tenure at the Tabernacle, the First Presidency opted instead to skirt the issue by leaving the post of "chief organist" vacant. Schreiner was not made "chief organist" until 1965 after Asper's retirement. Schreiner did not return to the Tabernacle as a full-time organist until 1939, having signed a contract with UCLA as university organist in the interim. Daniel Frederick Berghout and Kenneth Udy, *Alexander Schreiner: The California Years* (Harmonie Park Press, 2001).

11. Charles W. Nibley served as second counselor in the First Presidency at the time and was instrumental in convincing Schreiner to pursue the organ as a career.

12. Richard R. Lyman was a member of the Quorum of the Twelve Apostles. His wife Amy Brown Lyman was also influential in both church and civic capacities, serving in the Utah State Legislature and as the General Relief Society President as well as the first director of LDS Social Services. Schreiner married their daughter Margaret in 1927.

13. Tracy Cannon to Edward Kimball, May 13, 1930, Cannon Papers.

14. Ralph Taylor Cannon, "Remembrances, 1962," Cannon Papers.

extensively and were often asked to give dedicatory recitals on newly completed instruments, Cannon did not often perform solo recitals outside of the regular daily recitals in the Tabernacle. Cannon's final major recital took place on June 15, 1930, at the University of Chicago Chapel, where he was given an honorary Master of Music degree from the Chicago Musical College.[15] The letter from the college inviting Cannon to attend commencement exercises arrived in April during the Centennial Pageant. Cannon mentioned the honor in a letter to Kimball almost as an afterthought, an indication perhaps of the intense stress Cannon was under that spring. The local papers ran nearly simultaneous headlines in June, on the one hand announcing that Schreiner had succeeded Cannon as Tabernacle organist, while at the same time celebrating Cannon's success in Chicago.

Cannon's honorary degree was more than a performative gesture; though not a master's degree in the true sense, it helped to place Cannon on a level playing field with his peers at other institutions of higher learning. That he lacked a formal masters or doctoral degree seemed to be a sensitive subject for Cannon, particularly as his colleagues obtained advanced degrees (Robertson and Florence Madsen, both sought formal degrees after they had already been appointed chair of BYU's music department; Schreiner also obtained degrees after being already employed at UCLA and the University of Utah). In a letter to Ogden-area attorney Roy D. Thatcher, Cannon defended himself (and members of his McCune School faculty who also lacked advanced degrees) writing: "The custom of giving degrees was not in vogue during the time the majority of our teachers were studying. You will note that a number of them received diplomas, and I received an honorary masters degree. I am sure that the musical educational requirements of our teachers is excellent, and would merit masters and bachelors music degrees were they graduating at the present time."[16] Cannon also fielded many requests from early graduates of McCune who were in danger of losing their positions at other institutions because they did not have a bachelor's degree.

15. "Tracy Y. Cannon to Offer Organ Recital in Chicago," *Salt Lake Tribune*, June 8, 1930.

16. Tracy Cannon to Roy D. Thatcher, February 5, 1936, McCune School of Music and Art, 1925–1926, Special Collections, Harold B. Lee Library, Brigham Young University.

By 1931, Utah, like the rest of the nation, was deep in an economic depression. Enrollment at the McCune School suffered, reaching its lowest levels in years. Cannon accepted a small cut to his already meager salary as he struggled to keep the institution financially solvent. Cannon was made bishop over the Cannon Ward in 1931, an unpaid, lay leadership role in which Cannon assumed pastoral, organizational, and financial responsibility for the entire congregation. The ward had taken an ill-timed $50,000 loan in 1926 to construct a new meetinghouse, the congregation having outgrown the small chapel built by George Q. Cannon around 1897.[17] By the time Cannon assumed leadership, the congregation had paid all but $12,000 on the loan; however paying the remaining debt seemed an insurmountable task in the face of increasing unemployment within the congregation. Through a series of fundraisers, primarily dinners and concerts, as well as exacting frugality, Cannon was able to reduce the congregation's debt to $1,850 by 1934. A final push in the form of a pledge drive allowed Cannon to pay the loan in full and in 1935, the meetinghouse was finally dedicated, to Cannon's great relief.

In the midst of the Cannon Ward's fiscal strain, Cannon and Lettie faced financial turmoil of their own. Over the years they had managed, on Cannon's modest salary, to add an addition to their house to accommodate their seven children, build a small cabin at Wildwood Resort in Provo Canyon where the family vacationed, and even set aside a small nest egg held at Deseret National Bank in Salt Lake City. In early spring of 1932, Deseret National Bank succumbed to the same fate as thousands of other banks in the United States that failed during the Great Depression. The Cannons lost the entirety of their savings.

In 1935, tragedy again struck the Cannon household and Lettie died following a brief but acute period of illness. In the months after her death, Cannon reported that, "Life became very lonely and drab for me ... the thing that held me here was the responsibility I felt towards my children. I had now become both father and mother

17. By Cannon's account, the principal was only $40,000. *Cannon Ward in Retrospect: 1896–1946* (Church of Jesus Christ of Latter-day Saints, 1946).

to them and I wanted to carry out my responsibility to them in an acceptable manner."[18]

By this point, Cannon's two oldest boys were serving as church missionaries and the other children were nearing adulthood; however, the two youngest remained at home and needed daily parental support. One of Cannon's immediate concerns after Lettie's death was how he would continue to financially support his sons while also caring for the children still at home in Lettie's absence, as teaching extra music lessons in the evenings in order to fund the older boys' missions was no longer an option. Cannon's congregation stepped in to fill the void, collecting nearly $500 in support of the family, a gesture which deeply moved Cannon.

18. Carol Hinckley Cannon, "Tracy Y. Cannon: His Life and His Legacy," 1979, CHL.

CHAPTER NINE

"THE FINEST THING THE CHURCH HAS EVER DONE FOR MUSIC"

Heartbroken, Cannon poured himself into his work. In 1932, Gates had taught the first course for ward choristers at the McCune School; Cannon suggested that such a course could be expanded to include wards outside the Salt Lake City area, an idea which had been germinating since his Pioneer Stake Choristers and Organists Association days.[1] Unlike the annual organist and chorister training institutes which lasted only one day, Cannon's proposed training course would last several weeks, allowing students to progress through a series of lesson modules, resulting in a more thorough education than could possibly be achieved in a one-day training.

The General Music Committee first began discussing the logistics of such a training course in early 1927 when Cannon approached Adam Bennion, superintendent of the church's schools, about the prospect of using not only McCune but the church's other academies as training centers.[2] There was seemingly some confusion regarding not only who would administer the program, but also how it would be funded, and the plan was not revisited until 1935, when Cannon approached Grant requesting $600 to begin an experimental course to teach choristers and organists at the McCune School as a community outreach program for non-matriculating students. Cannon's request was granted.

1. In this context, the term chorister is analogous to choir director and refers to the individual who leads both the choir and congregational singing during an LDS worship service or meeting. This in contrast to other traditions where chorister refers to a member of a choir (often a student).

2. General Music Committee, "Meeting Minutes" (February 8, 1927), Music Files.

The following year, Cannon reached out again to the First Presidency, this time asking not only for additional funds, but an expanded reach for the program:

> Last fall you approved a suggestion that we give courses for choristers and organists at the McCune School of Music and Art. These courses were begun December 2, 1935, and have continued for seventeen weeks, there being eight lessons yet to be given. The enrollment is 105 choristers, and 96 organists.
>
> In these classes choristers are taught in groups of twenty and organists in groups of ten. The tuition for choristers is $5 each, for organists $10 each. Half of this amount was appropriated by the First Presidency, and the other half was paid by the wards. The students themselves bought their texts....
>
> The teaching of these classes has given us teachers much satisfaction because we have noted a very good improvement in their directing, and playing ability.... Inasmuch as we have found this deficiency in Salt Lake City where we would expect the best educated choristers and organists, we are much impressed with the need of extending this work to other districts outside of Salt Lake City.[3]

Cannon then suggested that the program be extended into the rest of Utah as well as Idaho using either local teachers (with the possibility of inferior instruction) or itinerant teachers (with the added financial burden of transportation and lodging). He estimated a total of 1,746 choristers and organists in the proposed areas, and therefore requested a $6,547 appropriation from the First Presidency to cover their portion of tuition costs (a total of 1,127 students actually enrolled during the 1936–1937 year).[4] Grant responded within the week, offering enthusiastic support as well as the requested funding.[5]

Ultimately the program used a combination of both local and itinerant instructors. The vast majority of the teachers had connections to the McCune School, either as faculty or former students, and included Cannon (organ), Asper (organ), LaMar Petersen (organ), J. J. Keeler (organ), Wade Stephens (organ), Lorenzo Mitchell (organ), Spencer Cornwall (chorister), Richard Condie (chorister), Franklin Madsen

3. Tracy Cannon to First Presidency, April 9, 1936, Music Files.
4. "Statement of Organists and Choristers Course, 1936–1937," McCune files.
5. Heber J. Grant to Tracy Cannon, April 17, 1936, Music Files.

(chorister), and Sterling Wheelwright (organ and chorister). During the first year classes were held in Salt Lake City, Provo and the surrounding area, Ogden, Logan, and in a number of towns in Idaho including Idaho Falls, Pocatello, Twin Falls, and Rexburg. The courses were attractive, as in many instances this was the only formal instruction ward choristers and organists had ever experienced:

> In every center this music educational program has been received with much enthusiasm. Many times the comment has been, "This is the finest thing the Church has ever done for church music." Bishops have told us of improved musical conditions in their wards. The students are practically unanimous in expressing the hope that the work will be continued, and their gratitude seems to have no bounds. The following incident will illustrate how eager the students were to receive the full benefit from the courses; last January when the temperature was 20 degrees below zero in Blackfoot [Idaho], a woman who lived three miles from the place where the class was being held, rode to and from the class on a horse.[6]

Given the success of the pilot program, Cannon requested additional funds in order to add a second year of coursework, as well as extend the program to stakes in Arizona, California, and Canada. In cases where stakes could not meet the minimum registration requirement to hold a twelve-week course, condensed one- or two-day institutes were conducted instead. The program was eventually expanded to include both a first-year course for beginners, and a second-year course for more advanced students.

Cannon's responsibilities both within the General Music Committee and the broader music community had increased gradually, and he eventually replaced Kimball as Melvin Ballard's assistant chair in 1937, following Kimball's untimely death.[7] In his new capacity as the committee's de facto community representative, Cannon (with characteristic optimism and sweeping grandiosity) gave the following address on KSL radio:

6. Tracy Cannon to First Presidency, April 1, 1937, Music Files.

7. Cannon's additional music leadership roles at this time included serving as member of the advisory committee for the Federal Music Project sponsored by the Works Progress Administration in 1936; serving on the board of the Utah State Institute of Fine Arts (which oversaw the newly formed Utah Symphony Orchestra); serving on the Utah Centennial Commission (which oversaw Utah's statehood centennial celebrations); and serving on the board of the Music Teacher's National Association.

> Our music ability, our artistic ability, or any natural aptitude is a gift from the Lord. Someday we will be held responsible for the development of these gifts. The Lord has blessed us with these abilities. Ours is the sacred duty of cultivating and exercising them for the blessing of mankind. We are a church that emphasizes the importance of the individual. Nevertheless, most of our work is done in groups—meetings, classes, and discussion circles. The truly thrilling element of our experience with music comes in watching the inspiration of music unite so large a group into a single heart. I think there is nothing so powerful in bringing together a group into one mind and one spirit as the singing of good songs. Under the inspiration of the Lord, our songs have become a powerful unifying element. Even in the hard pioneer days the leaders of the Church emphasized the cultural value of music and art. The difficult task of carrying a piano across the plains, the struggle of building a theater in the desert, the effort of seven long years to build the majestic organ of the Tabernacle—these bespeak a love and reverent regard for the softening, inspirational culture of music and art—a love and regard which the Church has always sought to cultivate among its membership and which it is today teaching more extensively than ever.[8]

Clearly, Cannon viewed the role of the church music committee as more expansive than the mere publication of hymnals; rather, he saw church music as integral to the construction of values, culture, and community throughout Utah (as well as the church's congregations outside the state). Possibly as a result of Cannon's vision, leadership skills, and standing in the community, when Ballard passed away in 1939, direction of the General Music Committee fell not to another apostle, but to Cannon.[9]

One of Cannon's first campaigns as committee chair was the initiation of a "hymn of the month" program to familiarize the membership with *Latter-day Saint Hymns* and to motivate congregations that had not yet acquired complete sets of the hymnal (thirteen years after its publication) to promptly do so. Performance instructions for hymn singing were given in the music column of *The Improvement Era*. For instance, regarding the hymn "Glory to God

8. Cannon, "Tracy Y. Cannon."

9. Marvin O. Ashton of the presiding bishopric was the general authority assigned to the General Music Committee from 1940 until his death in 1946. In 1940, Carol Hinckley (Cannon's secretary at the McCune School and later his third wife) was also assigned as the assistant secretary to the General Music Committee.

on High," Cornwall cautioned that: "This hymn is peculiar in that it contains two, three-measure phrases in the first line. The conductor should hasten the beats slightly in the final measure of each to ensure prompt attack on the first measures of the phrases following. This hymn should be sung in a stately manner—forte throughout. The tempo should neither be fast nor slow. A slight ritard may be introduced in the last two measures with good effect."[10]

Organists were given similarly detailed guidance, in this case proffered by Schreiner:

> The announcement by the organ should be forte, with octave couplers drawn, no tremolo, no celeste stops. It should be played in a bold, heroic manner without haste. Observe strictly the rests for breathing in number 113 as given.[11]

These are surprisingly thorough instructions for congregational singing; however, the program was based on the assumption that congregations would rehearse the hymns several times throughout the month during weekly auxiliary meetings before singing them in sacrament meeting, in addition to having support from the choir.

In 1939 Cannon had hired a new secretary at the McCune School, Caroline (Carol) Hinckley. Later Carol recalled her interview with Cannon:

> I first met Trace when I went to the McCune School to apply for a job as secretary. I walked into the school and the secretary directed me to sit and wait in the hall. It was not long before a very thin, white-haired man came briskly walking from the back of the hall to where I was sitting. He invited me into his studio. Trace's office and studio was a large room west of the main entrance of the building. It was a beautiful room with large mirrors on the walls. The walls were also paneled with beautiful tapestry in gold and rose. A life-size statue of Cleopatra stood in front of the largest wall mirror and there were two grand pianos and Trace's large, beautiful desk in the room.[12]

---

10. "Music," *The Improvement Era*. April 1940, 236.
11. "Music," *The Improvement Era*.
12. Many of Cannon's close friends and family called him "Trace." This description implies that at some point, Cannon's office was moved from the east side of the school to the room on the school's west side which originally had been used as the recital hall, probably following the completion of the stage in the room which had formerly housed the McCune's library. Cannon, "Tracy Y. Cannon."

Cannon was immediately taken with Carol. In addition to her role as secretary at the McCune School, she also worked as secretary to the General Music Committee, meaning that she and Cannon spent a considerable amount of time together. Though twenty-three years his junior, Cannon and Carol began courting. Carol struggled with the difference in their ages, and while she enjoyed spending time with Cannon, Carol was hesitant about marriage. Cannon remained doggedly persistent, writing:

> Sometimes my discouragement became almost unendurable. One night I knelt before the Lord and told Him I would not arise from my knees until I had some kind of assurance from Him that I was to persist. The Lord let me stay on my knees for quite awhile. But finally the answer came unmistakably into my mind. It was simply this, "Keep on as you are." Quite some time after this, when it seemed to me I was making no progress, I went to the Lord again. This time the answer was slower in coming, but when it did come it was, "Be patient with her."[13]

During his four-year courtship with Carol, Cannon was appointed to serve as chair of Salt Lake County's selective service board number 11 by Utah's governor, Henry Blood. Cannon had become acquainted with Blood during his time as a missionary in London, where Blood acted in a number of leadership capacities, including as president of the London conference of the British mission. Like many Utahns, Cannon felt the impact of the Second World War within his own home; one son and two sons-in-law served in the military, gasoline rationing (as well as a 1942 ban on church-related auto travel imposed by the First Presidency) hampered the work being done by the organist and chorister training program, and enrollment at the McCune School was frustratingly low. The McCune School had always struggled to maintain enrollment in its core courses, particularly harmony and musicianship, and occasionally the courses were dropped from its schedule due to lack of students. The economic plunge of the 1930s, followed closely by World War II caused a precipitous drop in matriculation. Much to Cannon's dismay, the school lost its NASM accreditation in 1942, in part because it was unable to fill core theory courses for the requisite

13. Cannon, "Tracy Y. Cannon Legacy."

two consecutive years.[14] Despite Cannon's diligent efforts, McCune was never readmitted to the association, thereby beginning its slow decline from an institution of higher learning to a preparatory academy whose primary focus was youth enrichment.[15]

14. "Constitution and By Laws, Specimen Examinations, Approved Curricula, Code of Ethics, Membership," in National Association of Schools of Music, 1936.

15. As an early member of the association as well as an officer (he was elected as NASM vice president from 1935–36 and again in 1939–40), Cannon was well acquainted with the association's bylaws as well as its leadership, but even this was not enough to re-secure the school's accreditation. See Sheila Barrows, "Historical Perspectives 1924–1999: National Association of Schools of Music Seventy-Fifth Anniversary," National Association of Schools of Music, 1999.

CHAPTER TEN

"THE PRESENT HYMNBOOK IS THE MOST UNIQUE OF ANY PUBLISHED"

In March 1943 Cannon was finally relieved of his duties as member of the Deseret Sunday School board, and the following month, he and Carol were married. After a brief honeymoon, the couple settled into a routine of work and home. Using the money from the sale of Cannon's house on 800 West and Carol's house in Provo, the couple purchased a home on Emerson Avenue in Salt Lake's more affluent east side. The church's policy at the time prohibited married women from full-time church employment and Carol had to forgo her job at the McCune School; however, she was permitted to work on a part-time basis as General Music Committee secretary. Carol proved to be a boon to Cannon's professional life, particularly as his health began to fail.

By 1943, discussions were already underway regarding the publication of a new hymnal, and the committee was given permission by the First Presidency to begin a preliminary survey of existing hymns. An advisory committee comprising Harold B. Lee, Spencer W. Kimball, Mark E. Petersen, and Joseph F. Smith (all general authorities rather than musicians) was appointed to assist with the project.[1] As reported by Cannon, "Each member of the committee was assigned to go through the LDS Hymn Book (green book) and mark each hymn as follows: accept, accept revised, doubtful, discard. The word of the classification [is] to be written [next to] the composer's name in the book itself."[2]

1. "General Music Committee Summary, 1920–1961," Cannon Papers.
2. Tracy Cannon to Marvin Ashton, June 10, 1943, Music Files.

At the first meeting of the advisory committee, it was decided that further consolidation was needed for the church's many auxiliary songbooks. *Deseret Sunday School Songs* and *Latter-day Saint Hymns* would be blended into a single hymnal for use in all adult meetings of the church. The committee also voted to publish a "junior songbook" for use in meetings of children and youth as well as a songbook for "special occasions."[3] Proofreaders and editors of the three books were asked to provide their services without compensation; however, contributors who wrote new hymn tunes were paid $10 per composition, which gave the church full ownership and copyright privileges.[4]

Whereas the focus of both the 1889 *Psalmody* and 1927 *Latter-day Saint Hymns* had been to cultivate locally created hymnody, the advisory committee for the revised hymnal made a complete policy reversal:

> It is planned in addition to these songs [from *Latter-day Saint Hymns* and *Deseret Sunday School Song Book*] to add a number of new songs from world-wide sources.... As a Committee we were impressed by the fact that some of our most beloved hymns were obtained from outside composers and writers. This has argued for the desirability of obtaining from similar sources other equally splendid songs that are now not included in our song literature.[5]

The committee delivered on this promise; the more parochial hymns from the 1927 hymnal were removed and a number of beloved hymns from mainstream Protestant Christendom that had previously been absent from the Mormon canon were added, including: "All Creatures of Our God and King," "Christ the Lord is Risen Today," and "Lord Dismiss Us With Thy Blessing." These hymns were carefully selected from several hymnals but primarily *The Hymnal of the Protestant Episcopal Church in the United States of*

3. The special occasion song book was published in 1949 and titled *Recreational Songs*. It included a variety of songs both secular and sacred such as folk songs (translated into English) from a variety of countries, songs for Christmas, and even a section dedicated to the works of Gilbert and Sullivan. The junior songbook would eventually be published in 1951 under the title *The Children Sing*.

4. Tracy Cannon to Leroy Robertson, August 30, 1947, Leroy Robertson Papers, Special Collections, Marriott Library, University of Utah.

5. Harold B. Lee, Spencer W. Kimball, and Mark E. Petersen to the First Presidency, October 25, 1944, Music Files.

America (1940) and *The Methodist Hymnal* (1939). Words were adjusted and some verses omitted entirely to bring the hymns into alignment with LDS doctrine.[6]

As the 1927 hymnal had helped to launch Robertson's compositional career, the revised one had a similar impact for other up-and-coming local composers, including J. J. Keeler and Crawford Gates (a distant relative of B. Cecil Gates), who were both Robertson's students at BYU. Gates's choral setting of "Ring Out Wild Bells" for the hymnal caught the attention of Cannon, who later recommended the young composer to the Utah Pioneer Centennial Pageant committee (headed by Cannon) as they searched for someone to score the play *Promised Valley*. Though the committee was wary of choosing a composer with so little experience (Gates was only twenty-eight at the time), Cannon successfully persuaded them to take a chance. The *Promised Valley* score was a success and signaled the start of a fruitful relationship for Gates with both Cannon as well as church leadership.[7]

The committee first set about collecting hymn texts. A hymn writing contest was once again sponsored by the *Deseret News*, taking the place of its annual Christmas poem contest. The newspaper offered a $25 grand prize for the best text (with $10 being given for any other texts the committee accepted for the hymnal). The following suggestions were given as guidance:

> 1. The words should be addressed to the Deity.
>
> 2. Subject matter should preferably be related to the present Gospel dispensation. Some may wish to write sacramental hymns, however, and these will be acceptable.
>
> 3. The opening phrase should be sufficiently strong to make a good title.
>
> 4. Stanzas should not be too long, and there should be a minimum of three stanzas in the song and a maximum of five.
>
> 5. Hymns without choruses are preferred.
>
> 6. Meters and accents must match perfectly.
>
> 7. Stanzas, while related to each other, should not necessarily be dependent upon each other.

6. General Music Committee, "Meeting Minutes" (November 19, 1944), Music Files.
7. Crawford Gates to Tracy Cannon, September 3, 1947, Cannon Papers.

> 8. A positive spirit of praise and uplift is desired, rather than merely a narrative style.[8]

A total of 590 submissions were received by the *Deseret News*, which was winnowed down to 150 options for consideration by the committee.

Once suitable texts were obtained, the following was then sent to local composers soliciting musical settings:

> Because of your knowledge of music composition we would like you to work with us in this project. We are seeking new music settings for the enclosed list of words. We hope you will choose from among them those that interest you.... All manuscripts should be sent in under a nom de plume, with the name and address of the composer enclosed in a sealed envelope.
>
> Based on the character of the hymns already submitted, we offer the following suggestions as a guide for your further study and effort:
>
> The hymn style must be adhered to in all compositions submitted.
>
> The melodic line must be strong and original and have definite appeal. Try always to avoid triteness.
>
> All common errors of harmonic progressions such as doubling of major thirds, unresolved dissonances, parallel fifths and octaves, cross relationships, unsingable uses of the tritone, wrong chords, in fact any signs of musical illiteracy should be entirely absent.
>
> Your constant query should be—"Am I producing a hymn which the people of the Church will enjoy singing and a hymn which they will sing often, without undue promotion?"
>
> We have many fine hymns in our repertoire now and those you write at the present time will naturally be in competition with the best of these. If our new hymns are to be sung, they must have in them some of the appeal which has made our present day hymns popular. You should make a diligent study of the vital elements of all great hymns and seek to incorporate them into your writings.[9]

The committee voted on forty-eight of the newly composed settings in December 1945. Because the pool of hymns included some by committee members, Cannon suggested that their manuscripts be mixed in with the non-committee member submissions. The text

8. "Deseret News Opens Hymn-Writing Contest," *Deseret News*, October 18, 1944.
9. Tracy Cannon, Letter dated August 1, 1945, Music Files.

of each hymn was read aloud, and then the hymn was played in its entirety by Schreiner. Committee members then marked each hymn as "accept" or "reject" along with any accompanying remarks. Cannon asked the committee to refrain from speaking or discussing the hymns during the selection process, so as to remain as unbiased as possible. Cannon contributed a number of hymn-settings to the new hymnal including: *Come, Rejoice* (Hinckley); *The Lord Be With Us* (Frances); *God of Power, God of Right* (Elsie); *How Beautiful Thy Temples, Lord* (Judith); *Jesus, Mighty King of Zion* (Viola); *Praise the Lord With Heart and Voice* (Rose Ann). Charmingly, Cannon named his hymn tunes after his wives, Elsie, Lettie (represented first in the 1927 hymnal, "Let Us Sing an Evening Hymn"), and Carol. Some flexibility was required for Carol's hymn, as the tune name CAROL was already in use; therefore her maiden name, Hinckley, was used instead. Cannon named the remaining tunes for his daughters, Frances, Judith, and Rose Ann, as well as Lettie's youngest sister, Viola.[10]

The committee determined to organize the adult hymnal into four sections of congregational hymns followed by arrangements for choirs, male voices, and female voices. While some hymns were included in only one section, others were rearranged and included in multiple sections. Even with the duplications, the new hymnal was much smaller than its 1927 counterpart, indicating just how many of the 1927 hymns were never fully embraced by church membership. In describing the four sections of the hymnal Cannon remarked:

> The present hymn book is the most utilitarian and unique of any hymn book yet published. To meet the needs of our various types of gatherings it is divided into four sections, one for mixed groups, one for priesthood meetings and one for gatherings of women. The other section consists of [other] hymns to be sung by ward choirs. These choir hymns are unique to our Church. They were written by our own early composers for the choirs they directed and differ from the traditional hymns in that their vocal range is greater and the music more florid.[11]

The work of arranging and editing selected hymns for female voices was given to Florence Jeppersen Madsen, who served on the

10. CAROL is the name of the tune associated with "It Came Upon a Midnight Clear."
11. Tracy Cannon, Speech given at MIA Conference, June 1959, Cannon Papers.

General Board of the Relief Society (which afforded her a place on the music committee) and also directed a women's church choir called the "Singing Mothers" that performed at the semiannual General Relief Society Conferences. Known for her egalitarian approach, Madsen believed everyone was capable of singing if given proper opportunity and training. As such, she carefully selected and arranged a total of forty-one hymns for women's voices, applying expertise acquired through years of work with female choruses.

As Cannon's first assistant on the General Music Committee, Robertson also edited a number of hymns. Both he and Madsen were on sabbatical from BYU and spending their time in Southern California.[12] Cannon had a hand in Robertson's leave of absence; unbeknownst to Robertson, Cannon petitioned the First Presidency to request that the BYU professor's teaching load be reduced so that he might be free to compose and tend to his work for the committee.[13] This level of deference continued to be extended while Robertson was in California; Cannon mailed hymn proofs to Robertson at considerable expense to the committee, seeking Robertson's approval of even minute details. Unfortunately, Madsen was not afforded the same consideration, as she expressed in a pointed letter to Cannon:

> When asked to arrange the numbers for the women's section, I realized that to do it I would have to use the three months leave (part of my Sabbatical leave) in order to do it. This of course meant that all the plans I had previously made had to be dropped. The work has been taxing on both eyes and nerves but I have done it willingly, realizing that it was for a worthy cause and was a call from the church.
>
> Yesterday when turning through the pages of the manuscript books I had sent you, I was surprised and very humiliated to find that my work had undergone many changes and revisions.
>
> I realize that there is always more than one way to do things, and one way may be just as good as another, however, the one whose responsibility

12. Robertson was earning a Ph.D. from the University of Southern California in addition to working on his oratorio *The Book of Mormon*. Madsen and her husband, Franklin, on the other hand, traveled to California numerous times so that Franklin could continue his studies. While there, the couple organized stake and ward choirs and provided training in conducting and choir leadership.

13. Tracy Cannon to First Presidency, December 15, 1944, and First Presidency to Franklin Harris, December 18, 1944, Music Files.

> it is to do the work ought to be allowed to chose his own style and idiom of expression. Am I not right?
>
> If it were thought expedient for all the manuscripts of the new song book to go through the hands of a specialized music editor, then I would say "well and good," but for one colleague in the same profession as another to edit and make changes of the other's work is rather unethical and humiliating.
>
> I was given no form to follow, therefore, I have used my own judgement in the work I have done. I feel I pretty well know what the singing groups can do, having worked with them throughout the years.... If you still feel that certain changes must be made, I shall be glad to make them in my own style, otherwise, I think it would be better to discard them altogether.[14]

Taking advantage of the Tabernacle's newly acquired sound equipment, quartets of singers and even ward choirs were asked to make recordings of hymn arrangements so that the committee (and more importantly, its non-musician advisors) might hear the hymns in context. This effort was spearheaded by J. Spencer Cornwall, who prepared the singers, accompanists, and perusal scores; the recordings were often made following the Tabernacle Choir's Sunday morning broadcasts.

By 1948 the new hymnal was completed and ready for printing. At the request of church president George Albert Smith, the hymnal was to be called *Hymns: The Church of Jesus Christ of Latter-day Saints.* Unlike the 1927 hymnal which was published with little fanfare, the committee celebrated the publication of the 1948 hymnal with numerous full-length articles, demonstrating that the church had gained a firmer understanding of the importance of public relations. An article ran in the *Deseret News* explaining not only the church's four new song collections to serve the various audiences of the church, but also described the adult hymnal's groupings (congregational, choir, men's voices, and women's voices), its new topical index with hymns arranged by both event (funeral, sacrament, etc.) and by gospel principle (a total of thirteen principles were included), and even an explanation of the Italian tempo marks that were now included at the start of each hymn. The article notes that:

14. Florence Madsen to Tracy Cannon, March 21, 1946, Music Files.

> Few hymn books in any church have as many hymns produced by its own members as the LDS book. An actual count reveals that 168 texts were written by Latter-day Saints, and 140 texts were written by non-members. The music for 165 of the hymns was composed by Latter-day Saint musicians, and the music of 143 hymns is the work of non-Latter-day Saints.[15]

This reveals that in spite of the advisory committee's commitment to importing more hymns from outside sources, the proportion of Mormon to non-Mormon derived hymns remained essentially the same as it had in the 1927 hymnal (but perhaps with a greater sense of focus). It also indicates that the music committee still believed a collection of hymnody perceived to be distinctively Mormon would be better received by the membership.

The new hymnal was stately, serene, and dignified, with settings reminiscent of Lutheran chorales. Largely absent were the "campy" hymns which were so prevalent in *Songs of Zion* and *Deseret Sunday School Songs.* While some church members appreciated the elegant, new hymn style, others missed the hymns of their youth. Again, a hymn-of-the-month program was scheduled to begin in January 1949 in order to encourage familiarity with the new hymnal. Unfortunately, it was quickly discovered that the hymnal was riddled with typographical errors as well as insufficient binding; a new edition was planned within months of the first version's release. The 1950 edition contained an additional three hymns along with improved formatting and binding. To announce the new edition, the committee held a hymn festival in the Salt Lake Tabernacle with congregational singing led by Cornwall and the Tabernacle Choir, with Schreiner at the organ. Cannon, Schreiner, Asper, and Robertson spoke about the process of composing hymns and everyone in attendance received a 55-page souvenir booklet.[16]

---

15. "Long-Awaited Song Book Now Off Press," *Deseret News,* September 22, 1948.
16. "S. L. Song Fest to Announce New Hymn Book," *Salt Lake Tribune,* January 7, 1951.

CHAPTER ELEVEN

"WHAT SHALL BE TAUGHT TO THE FIRST YEAR ORGANIST?"

Cannon's organist and chorister training program continued to be the General Music Committee's most impactful venture. By 1946, course fees were still $5 for choristers and $10 for organists for twenty-four total hours of instruction. Teachers were paid $3 per instructional hour. Itinerant teachers were reimbursed their mileage and expenses (a practice which was curtailed during the Second World War when all church-funded travel was suspended); however, insufficient funding was a perpetual problem. Mitchell wrote expressing his frustration to Cannon while on assignment in Denver:

> Expenses are very high. I am hoping to limit the expense to the amount of tuition collected. We have come a long way since I first taught for the Music Committee. Thirteen years ago, twenty-five dollars was more than sufficient for one week. Denver is the most expensive place I have ever visited. Hotel accommodation is five dollars per day for one person. We have taken a motel close to the church in which we teach thereby eliminating considerable mileage expense.[1]

The entire organist and chorister training program was overseen by the McCune School, including student registration, scheduling out-of-town courses, and instructor compensation.

Periodic inservice training was held for the instructors, which included discussion of administrative items such as compensation and record keeping as well as instructional strategies and workshops with titles such as "Planning to Use Every Minute of the Class Period"

1. Lorenzo Mitchell to Tracy Cannon, October 28, 1951, Music Files.

and "What Shall be Taught to the First Year Organist?"[2] Students wishing to obtain credit for their coursework from the McCune School were given a final examination which was then graded and returned to McCune's office. Certificates were given to students who successfully completed both years of the program, and bishops were encouraged to recognize these efforts during sacrament meeting.

The first year chorister course included basic instruction in conducting patterns, use of the baton, establishment of tempo, rehearsal planning, and diction and vocalization primarily in regard to hymn-singing. During the second year, students expanded these skills to include anthems and music for special groups such as men's chorus or women's chorus. First-year organists were taught the mechanics of the organ, legato versus staccato touch, the handling of repeated notes, organ fingering, and selecting proper music for LDS worship services. In the second year, students learned more advanced technique and registration, as well as creating arrangements and transcriptions and advanced hymn accompaniment.[3]

Eventually some sort of textbook for organists and choristers became necessary. Cannon was to asked to write lessons for organists that were reworked over the course of several years; Cannon's lessons began first as a pamphlet but later developed into a full-fledged organ method book, the first of its kind produced in Utah. Called *The Organist's Manual*, and first published by Deseret Book in 1937, the text was used to instruct church organists for several decades.[4]

Cannon's methodology is succinct, with only a few exercises to demonstrate each technique and is tailored specifically for a Mormon audience, referencing LDS hymns and using distinctively Mormon terminology such as "sacrament meeting." Cannon's book also provides a glimpse into organology peculiar to the first half of the twentieth century, as reed organs with relatively simple engineering were the norm in most chapels. The first edition contained no pedal exercises and was geared exclusively toward playing the

2. "Church Music Institute for Teacher," September 2–3, 1938, McCune files.

3. "Course Outline, 1938–1939," McCune files.

4. While the first publication date is listed as 1937, reference to *The Organist's Manual* under that title is made in *The Juvenile Instructor* as early as 1928. Serialized lessons by Cannon appeared in *The Juvenile Instructor* in 1922 under the title "Course for Organists."

reed organ. As more churches acquired either pipe or electronic organs with pedalboards, in 1952 Cannon added a section of pedal exercises to his text.[5] Cannon derived much of his approach to pedal instruction from the methodology of Pietro Yon, who had published his own *Organ Pedal Technic* in 1944; however, the exercises were entirely Cannon's.

In the final chapter of *The Organist's Manual*, Cannon suggests organ music appropriate for LDS services. In addition to considerations of occasion, suitability of the instrument, and the organist's skill-level, Cannon recommends the following regarding the appropriateness of the music:

> One danger of selecting pieces with captivating melodies is that many of them are now played in theatres and on the radio and have thus become associated with things secular, thereby arousing emotions other than religious.... The organist must be most discriminating in selecting the music he performs. The music selected should be devotional, impersonal and in harmony with the spirit of the Restored Gospel. Songs containing words which are contrary to the doctrines of the Latter-day Saints, such as *The Rosary, Ave Marias*, especially those that are well known, the hymn "Just As I Am Without One Plea," etc. should not be used. Music with lilting rhythms, dance forms, such as *The Gavotte* and *Minuet*, popular love songs, operatic selections, with the exceptions of some prayers such as "Elizabeth's Prayer" from *Tannhauser* are out of character and should not be used.[6]

Cannon's guidance as well as the organ and choral music recommended by the music committee promoted an expectation of dignity, refinement, and reverence expected at LDS services. Some ward organists ignored Cannon's instructions, and on more than one occasion, word reached the music committee that secular music was being played in sacrament meetings. Even committee members themselves found it difficult to resist doctrinally "unsound" or secular music; Schreiner included an arrangement of Mozart's *Ave Verum Corpus* in his first volume of *Organ Voluntaries* (which was intended for use by ward organists), and it seems he and his colleagues were tempted by "captivating melodies" and occasionally included

5. "'Organist's Manual' Okayed as Textbook," *Deseret News*, September 7, 1952.
6. Tracy Cannon, *The Organists Manual* (Deseret Book, 1937), 44–46.

selections that pushed the limit of Cannon's guidelines in the "special services for tourists" held in the Tabernacle on the first Sunday of each month.[7]

A textbook for choristers was first published sometime in the late 1940s: *Fundamentals of Conducting* by Cornwall. Like Cannon's text, it was oriented specifically toward LDS ward choristers, with the majority of its musical examples pulled from the hymnal.[8] In addition to basic conducting and rehearsal techniques, Cornwall's text also included explanations of beginning music theory (something *The Organist's Manual* lacked). In *Fundamentals of Conducting*, one could find an introduction to rhythmic notation, scales, and major/minor triads, which is a reminder that many ward choristers had only a rudimentary understanding of music theory and were not trained musicians. Nevertheless, Cornwall presumed that whatever his audience lacked in technical skill, they compensated with cultural proficiency; the text contains numerous references to European composers and conductors (Corelli, Beethoven, Berg, Meyerbeer, Toscanini, etc.) by last name only and with virtually no context as if Cornwall assumed his audience was already well-acquainted with the major figures in Western music. This was not the only instance of Cornwall writing beyond the comprehension of his audience. Cannon responded similarly to an article Cornwall wrote for one of the church's periodicals:

> I would like to discuss with you the article you sent on "What is Beauty in Tone Quality?" It is a very fine and learned article.... I am wondering, however, if it is too scholarly for many of our ward and stake directors.... What we are seeking to do is to give the ward choir directors some fairly simple suggestions that they, with their limited knowledge, can put into practice.[9]

In addition to the annual music institutes and the organist and chorister training program, the committee experimented with

7. These selections included Lefebure–Wely's *Hymn of the Nuns*, Bossi's *Ave Maria*, arrangements of love songs, and pieces that veered into the domain of secular such as Liszt's *Liebestraum, no. 3* and Schumann's *Romanza*. See "Recitals for Tourists," Tabernacle Recital Programs, CHL.

8. J. Spencer Cornwall, *Fundamentals of Conducting* (Deseret Book, 1958). Initial date of publication unknown.

9. Tracy Cannon to J. Spencer Cornwall, March 25, 1960, Music Files.

other methods of reaching organists and choristers, as logistically they could only conduct training in each stake every three to four years. As the church began to spread outward from its central hub in Salt Lake City, it became increasingly difficult to provide intensive trainings; the committee balked at the cost of sending itinerant instructors to distant congregations and few instructors warmed to the idea of being on the road for weeks or even months at a time. The committee thus turned to media in an attempt to reach its far-flung organists and choristers.

The committee first began mailing a periodic music bulletin to ward and stake leaders in 1920. The bulletins were written by members of the committee and offered practical strategies for such topics as congregational accompaniment, learning new repertoire in choir rehearsals, suggesting pieces for special events such as Christmas and Easter, and addressing performance anxiety— many of the same topics that students would encounter in the organist and chorister training course. The bulletin was also used to announce music festivals, newly published anthems, and hymns for monthly study. Sometimes the bulletins were earnest, intending to convey the serious nature of sacred music (and perhaps putting too many demands on the amateur ward musician): "Every rehearsal should first be educational—something must be learned. Second, every rehearsal should be inspirational and exhilarating. When singers are compelled to sing under the stress of tyrannical dictatorial harshness, exhilaration is seldom in evidence. Third, a rehearsal must always have a religious atmosphere—you are learning to sing sacred music."[10]

Other bulletins were more blithe:

> Do not bother yourselves too much about the difficulty of playing the pedal basses. Play them by all means when the music is stately and impressive, and when the bass line moves easily. But when the bass goes too high for your comfort, or moves too fast, leave out the pedals. Would you like more help? Then consult the music articles which appear monthly in *The Instructor.* Most of these give special technical suggestions to help you play the hymns well. Here is a secret: the magic lies in practicing after you read. I know it works. I have tried it.[11]

---

10. "Bulletin No. 5–61," Music Files.
11. "Bulletin 1957–58," Music Files.

Occasionally, matters of procedural importance made their way into the bulletin, which gives a glimpse into the kind of cultural experience the committee was attempting to create. Many of these guidelines echo those preached by Cannon in *The Organist's Manual*, with a few notable additions:

> Music used in the Sacrament meeting should be carefully chosen. Only music of definite spiritual content, which is in harmony with the spirit of the restored gospel is acceptable. If there is doubt about the spirituality of any music to be used, follow this rule: DON'T USE IT.
>
> Instrumental music should be used sparingly. When deemed proper, it should be limited preferably to the string instruments (violin, viola, cello, bass) and the organ.
>
> The organ is the Church instrument. The piano may appropriately be used for accompaniment for solos when necessary.
>
> It is appropriate for the congregation to sing the last hymn in the service, and possibly one other.
>
> The conducting officer may, if he chooses, read the first verse of the opening hymn when announcing it.
>
> The meeting is officially closed with the benediction. The congregation should not be asked to remain seated to listen to further music, either by the choir or the organist. The organist plays a postlude as the congregation leaves the chapel.[12]

Debates about the suitability of musical instruments for worship, as well as the type of pieces used during a worship were not limited to Mormonism; however, whereas most arguments within other sects regarding the sanction of music seemed to be related to adherence to interpretations of traditional biblical worship, the General Music Committee's primary concern was the creation of an atmosphere of quiet.

12. "Bulletin 5–62," Music Files.

CHAPTER TWELVE

"I BELIEVE I CAN LEAVE YOU A GOOD NAME"

Enrollment at the McCune School never recovered from its low during the Great Depression and Second World War. Losing its NASM accreditation and failing to come to a reciprocity agreement with the University of Utah meant that the McCune was in competition with the university's growing School of Music, rather than working in cooperation. By the 1940s McCune had been largely downgraded to a preparatory school, catering to children, youth, and community education, rather than matriculating students.

After suffering heart complications that required extensive recuperation, Cannon realized he lacked the energy necessary to revitalize the floundering McCune School and could no longer serve as both its director and as chair of the General Music Committee. Church leadership gave him the choice of which job to retain and Cannon opted to remain on the music committee, submitting his resignation as the school's director in the fall of 1950. Heartfelt appreciation poured in from the community, including colleagues, church leadership, and former students. A tribute banquet was held by the school to honor Cannon's twenty-five years of service. Writing to his long-time friend, composer Ernest Bloch, Cannon said cheerfully:

> The work I shall do now will not be difficult and will be much to my liking. The field is broad and offers a real challenge. It is the type of work in which my heart delights. One never likes to admit that his health is failing, but I had to resign from my duties at the school. However, the church people who employ me were very kind to me in many ways, so

> Carol and I shall be able to get along, even though it will be somewhat more difficult than formerly.[1]

Following Cannon's retirement, leadership of the McCune School was passed to N. Lorenzo Mitchell, an acolyte of Cannon and member of the General Music Committee. Mitchell struggled to find his footing. The school facilities were in desperate need of repair, enrollment continued to drop, and the school was no longer given extensive use of the Assembly Hall or Barratt Hall for rehearsals or concerts leaving it without a suitable concert venue. In 1952, the McCune School became officially affiliated with BYU and was rebranded the McCune School of Music and Art of Brigham Young University.

This determination was the work of Joseph B. Wirthlin, who was made the presiding bishop in 1952 and as such also served on the McCune School's board of trustees, along with Ernest Wilkinson, who had begun his tenure as president of BYU in 1951. Wilkinson envisioned a unified church educational system, with all of the church's junior colleges, academies, seminaries, and institutes of religion answering to the LDS Church Board of Education *and* the Board of Trustees of Brigham Young University. Under this proposed plan, junior colleges such as Ricks College, Dixie College, and Weber College, which began as church academies before coming under state ownership, would revert back to the church and serve as feeder schools for BYU. Ultimately, the proposal was defeated at the ballot box, and Wilkinson's Unified Church School System plan was weakened.

The boards of both the McCune School and BYU pressed ahead, and McCune was made part of BYU. Many on the board of trustees were skeptical that the rebranded school could meet the more rigorous accreditation standards at BYU. Wirthlin issued this devastating assessment: "The school was little more than a rental agency, leasing space to teachers, and a bookkeeping service for their accounts. Other than the Junior Symphony Orchestra which the school sponsored, it made little direct contribution to the cultural atmosphere of the community."[2]

---

1. Tracy Cannon to Ernest Bloch, November 14, 1950, Cannon Papers.
2. Ernest L. Wilkinson, *Brigham Young University: The First One Hundred Years*, Vol. 2 (BYU Press, 1975), 597–99.

To meet Brigham Young University's accreditation standards, only the faculty with either long tenure at McCune or the requisite higher degrees were permitted to teach for credit and for the first time, students were required to take an entrance exam prior to enrolling. While this could have been a godsend for McCune—by coming under BYU's umbrella, the school would in theory regain stability as an institution of higher learning—but Mitchell's repeated requests for additional funding were denied and the school rapidly declined.[3]

McCune's enrollment continued to plummet leading to its closure in August 1957, though it appears this decision was made unilaterally without consulting Mitchell. In response to a letter from a former student regarding the transfer of credit, Mitchell wrote, "We have been severed from the Brigham Young University since the first of the year (only we didn't know it), and in any event the school is being closed August 15."[4] The church's board of education cited the school's lack of financial success, the fact that it offered no religious instruction, and that it adhered to different procedures and policies than BYU.[5] Mitchell attempted to bring the institution into procedural alignment with BYU during his tenure and while some issues, such as the lack of religious instruction, could have been easily remedied, perhaps the greater concern was that McCune was a relic from an earlier era where the divide between sacred and secular was significantly narrower.

A *Deseret News* tribute to the McCune School best summarizes its impact on the broader community:

> Of all the palatial landmarks in Utah, the McCune home on North Main Street has stood for half a century with few if any peers.... For the generation from 1920 down to the present time, the McCune School of Music and Art has been the place where more than 30,000 students have gone to take their piano, organ, violin, dancing and art lessons. For every one of these students and their parents, and for the many brilliant artists who served on the faculty, August 31, 1957—the day

3. Lorenzo Mitchell, "Justification for 1955 Budget," Provo, Brigham Young University, 1955, 22.

4. Lorenzo Mitchell to Jack Bowman, June 17, 1957, McCune files.

5. Donald G. Schaefer, "Contributions of the McCune School of Music and Art to Music Education in Utah, 1917–1957" (master's thesis, Brigham Young University, 1962), 86.

> the famed cultural center will close—will also end another era. Passing by the beautiful mansion is sure to recall pleasant memories for these thousands for years to come. Though the McCune School will soon be closed, yet the school's spirit and high artistic standards for which it has stood will long live in countless homes, on unnumbered concert stages and in many art centers the world around.[6]

Cannon recorded surprisingly little of his reaction to learning of McCune's closure, noting in a single letter his gratitude for a banquet held by the Salt Lake Chamber of Commerce in honor of the McCune faculty's contributions to the city over the years, though he privately shared that he felt both the church and the community had suffered a great loss.[7] The McCune School dominated much of Cannon's professional career and personal life. His children recalled with fondness visiting Cannon at the school, where he kept a supply of chocolates in his desk or would take them for lunch at the nearby Lion House. Even in Cannon's other wide ranging civic duties, which included serving on the boards of numerous organizations, he was always associated with the McCune School, as he opted to tend to any and all business from his school office.

Following his retirement as the school's director, Cannon was able to give his full attention to the General Music Committee. In 1952, the committee turned back to the "choral classics" and approved a special edition of masterworks published by Hall and McCreary. Called *Sing unto God: Easy Anthems and Sacred Choruses for the Mixed Choir, Special Edition Printed for the Church of Jesus Christ of Latter-day Saints*, the anthology contained works such as "O Rest in the Lord" by Mendelssohn and "God So Loved the World" by Stainer. Other pieces such as Mozart's "Ave Verum" and Bach's "O Sacred Head Now Wounded" from the *St. Matthew Passion* were translated and adapted by the collection's editor, Ruth Heller, which made them suitable for Mormon audiences. A complimentary copy of the anthology, along with order forms (each book was priced at 75 cents), was sent to each stake music director.

Wards were encouraged to build not only a sufficient choral library, but an organ library as well. Early suggestions included *Classic*

6. "No More McCune Concerts Either," *Deseret News,* June 17, 1957.
7. Tracy Cannon to Gus Backman, September 3, 1957, Cannon Papers.

and Modern Gems for the Reed Organ (Theodore Presser, 1899), *Reed Organ Playing* (Theodore Presser, 1914), and the four-volume *Vox Organi* (edited by Dudley Buck, 1896) as well as its reed organ counterpart, *Laus Organi.* Later the Tabernacle organists released their own anthologies of suitable organ music for LDS worship. Three volumes of organ pieces "compiled, edited, and composed" by Schreiner called *Organ Voluntaries* were published in 1937, 1945, and 1967. The pieces were devotional in nature and aside from compositions by Schreiner, were not exclusively Mormon. Schreiner favored the chorales of Bach (with anglicized titles), Mendelssohn, and Guilmant, and included excerpts of larger works and arrangements of well-known piano works. Asper also compiled a similar collection in 1942 called the *Devotional Pipe Organ Album,* and *The Organ in Church* in 1956; both books contained pieces of a similar nature to Schreiner's and would be appropriate for any Christian worship service, not just LDS sacrament meetings.

Perhaps the most innovative way that the committee attempted to guide choristers and organists was a set of three LP recordings with lessons and listening examples. The first record, *The Latter-day Saint Ward Organist*, was recorded by Schreiner in 1958. On the recording, Schreiner performs hymns, such as "Come, Come Ye Saints" with narration explaining the particularities of congregational accompaniment. The committee released a second record, *The Latter-day Saint Ward Choir*, the following year. A third record, *The Sunday School Organist,* was released in 1967. It contained seven anthems performed (and punctuated with Schreiner's narration) by a "typical ward choir with the same problems that confront many ward choirs throughout the Church," including: "How Beautiful Upon the Mountains" (Harker); "The Lord's Prayer" (Gates); "The Gospel Is Truly the Power of God" (Schreiner); "Jerusalem, O Turn Thee to the Lord" (Gonoud); "Seek Ye the Lord" (Roberts-Cornwall); "The Lord Will Comfort Zion" (Careless); and "Ye Simple Souls Who Stray" (Stephens).[8] The recordings are unique in that they contain poor examples, which

8. "Bulletin 3–59," Music Files.

after discussion by Schreiner, are then performed in the desired manner. The records could be ordered for $2.50 each.

Wards and stakes needed guidance not only for stocking their music libraries but in purchasing organs. During the first half of the twentieth century, each ward was responsible for procuring and maintaining its own instruments, a task that overwhelmed uninformed bishops, particularly when at the mercy of unscrupulous instrument dealers. The committee was therefore frequently called upon to make recommendations, interface with manufacturers, and provide assessments of already installed instruments. It was the practice of the committee to give broad recommendations, rather than maintaining allegiance to any one manufacturer, but they did remain rather staunchly opposed to electronic instruments. From a practical and financial standpoint, electronic organs provided an innovative approach to issues of cost and maintenance; however, the committee felt they were tonally unsatisfactory: "It was the opinion of the committee that the Estey reed organ (model 98) was superior to any of the electronic organs now available and that a small pipe organ was superior to any of the larger electronic organs."[9]

The committee was also concerned that the unproven electronic organs would have a short life expectancy and need frequent replacement. Any instruments purchased by a ward were first to be approved by the church's purchasing department after which a fixed appropriation would be given from the general church fund. The ward was responsible for any additional amount beyond the appropriation. Wards were encouraged to be frugal and in the case of chapels with a seating capacity of 150 or less, were directed to purchase a reed organ.[10]

The physical placement of organs in chapels was also an issue of concern for the committee. Cannon met with a group of architects along with the Presiding Bishopric and recommended that there should be some sort of architectural consistency from chapel to chapel; that the choir and organ should face the congregation (rather than being placed at the rear as is often the case in European churches); that provisions should be made to accommodate a

9. General Music Committee, "Meeting Minutes" (November 30, 1949), Music Files
10. First Presidency to Stake Presidents, January 20, 1950, Music Files.

pipe organ in any newly constructed chapels, even if the ward did not have funding to purchase an organ at that time; and that ample space and lighting should be provided for the choir and other musicians.[11] The committee recommended that pianos and organs be tuned at least every six months, a challenge for more rural areas where qualified technicians were not always readily available.

Music committee meetings were sporadic as Cannon convalesced following a heart attack in 1955; in a letter to friends, he wrote that he was "able to work only occasionally and for short periods of time."[12] Cannon became increasingly introspective, perhaps the result of the considerable time he spent at home recuperating. He began to write letters to his children:

> As I grow older and as life's shadows begin to come in the evening of life, I have many reflections. I am sure you will have them someday as I have them now. I want you to know that I love you all. I feel I have been honored by you, and that you always honored me … my life has been one of happiness and joy. There has been some great sorrow in it, as you know, but all in all I have been blessed above all … I can't leave you money. I believe, though, I can leave you a good name. I think that's about the best inheritance one can receive from a parent. That's what I am trying to leave you, a good name.[13]

By 1956, Cannon had recovered sufficiently to return to regular work though with a "shorter fuse" made evident in numerous letters he penned in frustration to committee members who failed to attend meetings or complete their assignments. As the capstone to Cannon's musical career, in 1957 he received word that the combined BYU choirs and orchestra would premiere his anthem written some years earlier entitled *O God Where Art Thou* (with text derived from section 121 of the *Doctrine and Covenants*). Cannon had originally scored the anthem for organ accompaniment, and Crawford Gates (who was by then teaching in BYU's music department) agreed to create an orchestration. Cannon was quite touched by his inclusion in the school's repertoire that semester alongside Haydn,

11. General Music Committee, "Meeting Minutes" (October 10, 1941), Music Files.
12. Tracy Cannon to "Wilf and Delores," December 5, 1955, Cannon Papers.
13. Tracy Cannon to children, 1951, Cannon Papers.

Buxtehude, Vaughan Williams, and Randall Thompson.[14] The anthem was scheduled for performance on May 27, 1958, in the field house at BYU, but the choral performance was canceled. Cannon expressed dismay and wondered if the anthem was too difficult—John Halliday of the music department had noted its chromaticism which made it challenging for young singers to learn.[15] Eventually it was performed on November 7, 1958 with Cannon and his family in attendance.

Despite recognition from the community, Cannon was rather modest about his compositions, writing:

> The hymns I have written that I like best are "Come Rejoice," "Praise the Lord with Heart and Voice," "Come, Let Us Sing an Evening Hymn," and "God of Power, God of Might." There is no special event which inspired me to write these hymns. I wrote them for inclusion in our present hymn book. My only thought was to make a contribution of praise to the Lord through music. I have also written some M.I.A. songs and some of them are found in the recreation song book. Also, I have written several anthems. The anthem I like best is a setting of "O My Father."[16]

And in response to a BYU student several years later:

> It is difficult to say which of my hymns is my favorite ... "God of Power, God of Right" and also "Come Rejoice" are perhaps among the best I have written.... The music of "Come, Rejoice" was written before the words. It so happens that music comes to me much easier than words. In this case I wrote words to fit the music, after the music was composed. However, this is an unusual procedure.[17]

Not long after the BYU premiere of his anthem, Cannon's health continued to decline until he was mostly bedridden with anemia and a chronic heart condition which required treatment with oxygen. The church offered no retirement plan, so Cannon remained as the General Music Committee chair, aided by Carol who continued to go into the office and bring home his correspondence. Cannon died

14. Tracy Cannon to Crawford Gates, January 10, 1958, Cannon Papers.
15. John Halliday to Tracy Cannon, March 11, 1958, Cannon Papers.
16. Tracy Cannon to Leon Paice, October 22, 1951, Cannon Papers.
17. Tracy Cannon to Gaye Marchant, November 1, 1956, Cannon Papers.

peacefully in his home on November 6, 1961, at the age of eighty-two. His funeral was held in the Assembly Hall on Temple Square. It was well attended and featured members of the Tabernacle Choir performing some of his own compositions. Cannon was remembered as thoughtful, quiet, soft-spoken, kind, and cultured and was lauded for his many contributions to the music of the church, particularly the organist and chorister training, which was estimated to have served 17,000 students during his tenure.[18]

Robertson was appointed as the new music committee chair in 1962 and Carol was asked to remain as committee secretary. The committee's goals and agenda remained much the same during Robertson's tenure: promote the hymns and congregational singing, nurture choirs, support and educate local music leadership in their roles, and dispatch a steady stream of recommendations for the church as a whole. This came to an abrupt halt in 1969 when church president David O. McKay announced that the General Music Committee would be replaced by a series of specialized ad hoc advisory committees. By this point, the organist and chorister education program had begun to disintegrate, challenged by serving the church's increasingly global footprint; local organist training had been largely turned over to BYU, which petitioned to open its own group organ instruction program in 1965.[19]

---

18. Harold Lundstrom, "Tracy Y. Cannon Paid Tribute for Advancing LDS Music Program," *Deseret News*, November 11, 1961.

19. Earl Crockett to Leroy Robertson, December 15, 1965, Leroy Robertson Papers.

EPILOGUE

As a musician, teacher, and administrator, Tracy Cannon guided the musical voice of Mormonism from its provincial roots into a state of decorous maturity. Cannon, though quiet and unassuming, was a cultural ambassador who dictated not only how outsiders came to understand the Church of Jesus Christ of Latter-day Saints, but also how church members understood themselves.

Like so many of his colleagues, both musician and non-musician, Cannon received his own musical training outside of Utah—in Michigan, Berlin, and Paris—as advanced musical instruction was virtually impossible to obtain within the state in the early twentieth century. For much of Utah's early statehood, higher education was essentially an import. The McCune School of Music and Art which opened around 1920, provided students with a conservatory education close to home, eliminating the need to travel to Europe to receive advanced training. Under Cannon's leadership, McCune became a cultural hub, offering accredited music degrees as well as community enrichment activities, and influencing Utah's next generation of music educators, composers, leaders, and policymakers.

Perhaps Cannon's most lasting legacy was his work with the General Music Committee of the Church of Jesus Christ of Latter-day Saints through which he oversaw the production of two hymnals, many anthem books, organ anthologies, method books, and an expansive organist and chorister education program. From the establishment of the General Music Committee in 1920 until Cannon's death in 1961, Mormon hymnody, which began as an idiosyncratic medium with "homespun" flare, developed into something refined, dignified, and emblematic of a people who had come to value reverence, social propriety, and moral exactness. Albeit some may argue, as Sterling Wheelwright did in his 1943 dissertation, that Mormonism's strength was in its eccentricity and that by diluting its homespun hymnody, Mormonism had essentially disrupted enthusiasm for hymn singing.[1]

A retroactive view demonstrates, however, that such an individualistic body of hymns as was found in LDS hymnody of the late nineteenth and early twentieth centuries would have been unlikely to survive the church's global expansion in the 1970s and 1980s. The 1985 hymnal for instance shows that a certain amount of Utah-centricity (e.g., references to the Western landscapes, etc.) must be sacrificed in order to appeal to a global audience. Indeed the very musical values Cannon sought to instill were extremely white and Eurocentric, relying on cultural competency that was unattainable even for many Utahns, let alone church members residing in other parts of the world.

Cannon's musical career was the climax for high art sacred music within the LDS Church, with an emphasis on post-Reformation European choral and organ masterworks, choral societies, order, and refinement. Cannon's "imported" tastes became the expected norm for LDS sacrament meetings and cultural events as the church found its place within broader society—a sort of Neo-Protestant Mormonism that imbued classical forms such as the oratorio, cantata, chorale, hymn, and anthem with Mormon dogma and theology.

Lowell Durham posed the question in 1968 (at the end of the high art period of Mormonism), "Is there a Mormon music?" Only 28% of his respondents, many of whom were members of the General Music Committee, answered in the affirmative.[2] They instead referred to the Mormon proclivity for "borrowing" music (such as hymn tunes and texts and forms such as the cantata), arguing that because the LDS Church lacks a musical form analogous to the Gregorian chant of the Roman Catholic Church, it lacks a distinctive musical heritage. What

1. Sterling Wheelwright, "The Role of Hymnody in the Development of the Latter-day Saint Movement," (PhD diss., University of Maryland, 1943).

2. Lowell Durham, "On Mormon Music and Musicians," *Dialogue: A Journal of Mormon Thought* 3, no. 4 (1968).

the respondents failed to recognize, however, is that Gregorian chant was not only borrowed from other sources (primarily Judaism and the Eastern Church) but that the Catholic Church was itself in a state of musical flux during the 1960s, resulting in an increasing number of cradle-Catholics who were wholly unfamiliar with Gregorian chant. Defining Catholic music by one single strand of influence would be imprudent.

This same logic applies to the music of Mormonism, itself a very young religion and certainly subject to additional growth and change. The Mormon musical voice has been governed by a number of influences including doctrinal priorities, personal preference, and the ability to communicate effectively with an ever-changing demography. During the first half of the twentieth century, Mormonism shed many of the vestiges of its polygamous, millennialist, frontier past and had not yet grappled with the challenges of creating a musical institution that could thrive in a church with increasing cultural diversity. The result was a "Camelot" of high art sacred music, heavily influenced by European taste and a desire for refinement and civility.

INDEX